RAPHAEL'S
HORARY ASTROLOGY

BY WHICH EVERY
QUESTION RELATING TO THE
FUTURE MAY BE ANSWERED

By

RAPHAEL

INCLUDING AN
INTRODUCTION ON ASTOLOGY

First published in 1931

Read & Co.

Copyright © 2022 Read & Co. Books

This edition is published by Read & Co. Books,
an imprint of Read & Co.

This book is copyright and may not be reproduced or copied in any
way without the express permission of the publisher in writing.

British Library Cataloguing-in-Publication Data
A catalogue record for this book is available
from the British Library.

Read & Co. is part of Read Books Ltd.
For more information visit
www.readandcobooks.co.uk

ASTROLOGY

By Morris Jastrow

The ancient art or science of divining the fate and future of human beings from indications given by the positions of the stars (sun, moon and planets). The belief in a connection between the heavenly bodies and the life of man has played an important part in human history. For long ages astronomy and astrology (which might be called astromancy, on the same principle as "chiromancy") were identified; and a distinction is made between "natural astrology," which predicts the motions of the heavenly bodies, eclipses, &c., and "judicial astrology," which studies the influence of the stars on human destiny. Isidore of Seville (d. 636) is one of the first to distinguish between astronomy and astrology; nor did astronomy begin to rid itself of astrology till the 16th century, when, with the system of Copernicus, the conviction that the earth itself is one of the heavenly bodies was finally established. The study of astromancy and the belief in it, as part of astronomy, is found in a developed form among the ancient Babylonians, and directly or indirectly through the Babylonians spread to other nations. It came to Greece about the middle of the 4th century B.C., and reached Rome before the opening of the Christian era. In India and China astronomy and astrology are largely reflections of Greek theories and speculations; and similarly with the introduction of Greek culture into Egypt, both astronomy and astrology were actively cultivated in the region of the Nile during the Hellenistic and Roman periods. Astrology was further developed by the Arabs from the 7th to the 13th century, and in the Europe of the 14th and 15th centuries astrologers were dominating influences at court.

Even up to the present day men of intellectual eminence like Dr Richard Garnett have convinced themselves that astromancy has a foundation of truth, just as there are still believers in chiromancy or other forms of divination. Dr Garnett ("A. G. Trent") insisted indeed that it was a mistake to confuse astrology with fortune-telling, and maintained that it was a "physical science just as much as geology," depending like them on ascertained facts, and grossly misrepresented by being connected with magic. Dr Garnett himself looked upon the study of biography in relation to the casting of horoscopes as an empirical investigation, but it is difficult in practice to keep the distinction clear, to judge by present-day text-books such as those of Dr Wilde (*Primer of Astrology*, &c.). Dr Wilde insists on there being "nothing incongruous with the laws of nature in the theory that the sun, moon and stars influence men's physical bodies and conditions, seeing that man is made up of a physical part of the earth." There is an obvious tendency, however, for astromancy to be employed, like palmistry, as a means of imposing on the ignorant and credulous. How far the more serious claim is likely to be revived in connexion with the renewal of research into the "occult" sciences generally, it is still too early to speculate; and it has to be recognized that such a point of view is opposed to the generally established belief that astrology is either mere superstition or absolute imposture, and that its former vogue was due either to deception or to the tyranny of an unscientific environment. But if the progress of physical science has not prevented the rehabilitation of much of ancient alchemy by the later researches into chemical change, and if psychology now finds a place for explanations of spiritualism and witchcraft which involve the admission of the empirical facts under a new theory (as in the case of the divining-rod, &c.), it is at least conceivable that some new synthesis might once more justify part at all events of ancient and medieval astromancy, to the extent of admitting the empirical facts where provable, and substituting for the supposed influence of the stars as such, some deeper theory which would be consistent with an application to other forms of prophecy, and thus might reconcile the possibility of dipping into futurity with certain interrelations of the universe, different indeed from those assumed by astrological theory, but underlying and explaining it. If this is ever accomplished it will need the patient investigation of a number of empirical observations by competent students unbiassed by any *parti pris*—a difficult set of conditions to obtain; and even then no definite results may be achieved.

The history of astrology can now be traced back to ancient Babylonia, and indeed to the earliest phases of Babylonian history, *i.e.* to about 3000 B.C. In Babylonia as well as in Assyria as a direct offshoot of Babylonian culture (or as we might also term it "Euphratean" culture), astrology takes its place in the official cult as one of the two chief means at the disposal of the priests (who were called *bārē* or "inspectors") for ascertaining the will and intention of the gods, the other being through the inspection of the liver of the sacrificial animal. Just as this latter method of divination rested on a well-defined theory, to wit, that the liver was the seat of the soul of the animal and that the deity in accepting the sacrifice identified himself with the animal, whose "soul" was thus placed in complete accord with that of the god and therefore reflected the mind and will of the god, so astrology is based on a theory of divine government of the world, which in contrast to "liver" divination assumes at the start a more scientific or pseudo-scientific aspect. This theory must be taken into consideration as a factor in accounting for the persistent hold which even at the present day astrology still maintains on many minds. Starting with the indisputable fact that man's life and happiness are largely dependent upon phenomena in the heavens, that the fertility of the soil is dependent upon the sun shining in the heavens as well as upon the rains that come from heaven, that on the other hand the mischief and damage done by storms and inundations, to both of which the Euphratean Valley was almost regularly subject, were to be traced likewise to the heavens, the conclusion was drawn that all the great gods had their seats in the heavens. In that early age of culture known as the "nomadic" stage, which under normal conditions precedes the "agricultural" stage, the moon cult is even more prominent than sun worship, and with the moon and sun cults thus furnished by the "popular" faith it was a natural step for the priests, who correspond to the "scientists" of a later day, to perfect a theory of a complete accord between phenomena observed in the heavens and occurrences on earth.

If moon and sun, whose regular movements conveyed to the more intelligent minds the conception of the reign of law and order in the universe as against the more popular notion of chance and caprice, were divine powers, the same held good of the planets, whose movements, though more difficult to follow, yet in the course of time came to be at least partially understood. Of the planets five were recognized—Jupiter, Venus, Saturn, Mercury and Mars—to name them in the order in which they appear in the older cuneiform literature; in later texts Mercury and Saturn change places. These five planets were identified with the great gods of the pantheon as follows:—Jupiter with Marduk, Venus with the goddess Ishtar, Saturn with Ninib, Mercury with Nebo, and Mars with Nergal. The movements of the sun, moon and five planets were regarded as representing the activity of the five gods in question, together with the moon-god Sin and the sun-god Shamash, in preparing the occurrences on earth. If, therefore, one could correctly read and interpret the activity of these powers, one knew what the gods were aiming to bring about. The Babylonian priests accordingly applied themselves to the task of perfecting a system of interpretation of the phenomena to be observed in the heavens, and it was natural that the system was extended from the moon, sun and five planets to the more prominent and recognizable fixed stars.

That system involved not merely the movements of the moon, sun and planets, but the observation of their relative position to one another and to all kinds of peculiarities noted at any point in the course of their movements: in the case of the moon, for instance, the exact appearance of the new crescent, its position in the heavens, the conditions at conjunction and opposition, the appearance of the horns, the halo frequently seen with the new moon, which was compared to a "cap," the ring round the full moon, which was called a "stall" (*i.e.* "enclosure"), and more of the like. To all these phenomena some significance was attached, and this significance was naturally intensified in the case of such a striking phenomenon as an eclipse of the moon. Applying the same method of careful observation to the sun and planets, and later to some of the constellations and to many of the fixed stars, it will be apparent that the body of observations noted must have grown in the course of time to large and indeed to enormous proportions, and correspondingly the interpretations assigned to the nearly endless variations in the phenomena thus observed. The interpretations themselves were based (as in the case of divination through the liver) chiefly on two factors:—(1) on the recollection or on written records of what in the past had taken place when the phenomenon or phenomena in question had been observed, and (2) association of ideas—involving sometimes merely a play upon words—in connexion with the phenomenon or phenomena observed. Thus if on a certain occasion the rise of the new moon in a cloudy sky was followed by victory over an enemy or by abundant rain, the sign in question was thus proved to be a favourable one and its recurrence would be regarded as a good omen, though the prognostication would not necessarily be limited to the one or the other of those occurrences, but might be extended to apply to other circumstances. On the other hand, the appearance of the new moon earlier than was expected was regarded as an unfavourable omen—prognosticating in one case defeat, in another death among cattle, in a third bad crops—not necessarily because these events actually took place after such a phenomenon, but by an application of the general principle resting upon association of ideas whereby anything premature would suggest an unfavourable occurrence. A thin halo seen above the new moon was pictured as a cap, and the association between this and the symbol of royalty, which was a conical-shaped cap, led to interpreting the phenomenon as an indication that the ruler would have a successful reign. In this way a mass of traditional interpretation of all kinds of observed phenomena was gathered, and once gathered became a guide to the priests for all times.

Astrology in this its earliest stage is, however, marked by two characteristic limitations. In the first place, the movements and position of the heavenly bodies point to such occurrences as are of public import and affect the general welfare. The individual's interests are not in any way involved, and we must descend many centuries and pass beyond the confines of Babylonia and Assyria before we reach that phase which in medieval and modern astrology is almost exclusively dwelt upon— genethliology or the individual horoscope. In Babylonia and Assyria the cult centred largely and indeed almost exclusively in the public welfare and the person of the king, because upon his well-being and favour with the gods the fortunes of the country were dependent in accordance with the ancient conception of kingship (see J. G. Frazer, *The Early History of Kingship*). To some extent, the individual came in for his share in the incantations and in the purification ritual through which one might hope to rid oneself of the power of the demons and of other evil spirits, but outside of this the important aim of the priests was to secure for the general benefit the favour of the gods, or, as a means of preparing oneself for what the future had in store, to ascertain in time whether that favour would be granted in any particular instance or would be continued in the future. Hence in "liver" divination, as in astrology, the interpretations of the signs noted all have reference to public affairs and events and not to the individual's needs or desires. In the second place, the astronomical knowledge presupposed and accompanying early Babylonian astrology is essentially of an empirical character. While in a general way the reign of law and order in the movements of the heavenly bodies was recognized, and indeed must have exercised an influence at an early period in leading to the rise of a methodical divination that was certainly of a much higher order than the examination of an animal's liver, yet the importance that was laid upon the endless variations in the form of the phenomena and the equally numerous apparent deviations from what were regarded as normal conditions, prevented for a long time the rise of any serious study of astronomy beyond what was needed for the purely practical purposes that the priests as "inspectors" of the heavens (as they were also the "inspectors" of the sacrificial livers) had in mind. True, we have, probably as early as the days of Khammurabi, *i.e. c.* 2000 B.C., the combinations of prominent groups of stars with outlines of pictures fantastically put together, but there is no evidence that prior to 700 B.C. more than a number of the constellations of our zodiac had become part of the current astronomy. The theory of the ecliptic as representing the course of the sun through the year, divided among twelve constellations with a measurement of 30° to each division, is also of Babylonian origin, as has now been definitely proved; but it does not appear to have been perfected until after the fall of the Babylonian empire in 539 B.C. Similarly, the other accomplishments of Babylonian astronomers, such as their system or rather systems of moon calculations and the drawing up of planetary tablets, belong to this late period, so that the golden age of Babylonian astronomy belongs not to the remote past, as was until recently supposed, but to the Seleucid period, *i.e.* after the advent of the Greeks in the Euphrates Valley. From certain expressions used in astrological texts that are earlier than the 7th century B.C. it would appear, indeed, that the beginnings at least of the calculation of sun and moon eclipses belong to the earlier period, but here, too, the chief work accomplished was after 400 B.C., and the defectiveness of early Babylonian astronomy may be gathered from the fact that as late as the 6th century B.C. an error of almost an entire month was made by the Babylonian astronomers in the attempt to determine through calculation the beginning of a certain year.

The researches of Bouché-Leclercq, Cumont and Boll have enabled us to fix with a considerable degree of definiteness the middle of the 4th century B.C. as the period when Babylonian astrology began its triumphal march to the west, invading the domain of Greek and Roman culture and destined to exercise a strong hold on all nations and groups—more particularly in Egypt—that came within the sphere of Greek and Roman influence. It is rather significant that this spread of astrology should have been concomitant with the intellectual impulse that led to the rise of a genuine scientific phase of astronomy in Babylonia itself, which must have weakened to some extent the hold that astrology had on the priests and the people. The advent of the Persians, bringing with them a conception of religion of a far higher order than Babylonian-Assyrian polytheism, must also have acted as a disintegrating factor in leading to the decline of the old faith in the Euphrates Valley, and we thus have the interesting though not entirely exceptional phenomenon of a great civilization bequeathing as a legacy to posterity a superstition instead of a real achievement. "Chaldaean wisdom" became among Greeks and Romans the synonym of divination through the planets and stars, and it is not surprising that in the course of time to be known as a "Chaldaean" carried with it frequently the suspicion of charlatanry and of more or less wilful deception. The spread of astrology beyond Babylonia is thus concomitant with the rise of a truly scientific astronomy in Babylonia itself, which in turn is due to the intellectual impulse afforded by the contact with new forms of culture from both the East and the West.

In the hands of the Greeks and of the later Egyptians both

astrology and astronomy were carried far beyond the limits attained by the Babylonians, and it is indeed a matter of surprise to observe the harmonious combination of the two fields—a harmony that seems to grow more complete with each age, and that is not broken until we reach the threshold of modern science in the 16th century. To the Greek astronomer Hipparchus belongs the credit of the discovery (*c.* 130 B.C.) of the theory of the precession of the equinoxes, for a knowledge of which among the Babylonians we find no definite proof; but such a signal advance in pure science did not prevent the Greeks from developing in a most elaborate manner the theory of the influence of the planets upon the fate of the individual. The endeavour to trace the horoscope of the individual from the position of the planets and stars at the time of birth (or, as was attempted by other astrologers, at the time of conception) represents the most significant contribution of the Greeks to astrology. The system was carried to such a degree of perfection that later ages made but few additions of an essential character to the genethliology or drawing up of the individual horoscope by the Greek astrologers. The system was taken up almost bodily by the Arab astronomers, it was embodied in the Kabbalistic lore of Jews and Christians, and through these and other channels came to be the substance of the astrology of the middle ages, forming, as already pointed out, under the designation of "judicial astrology," a pseudo-science which was placed on a perfect footing of equality with "natural astrology" or the more genuine science of the study of the motions and phenomena of the heavenly bodies.

Partly in further development of views unfolded in Babylonia, but chiefly under Greek influences, the scope of astrology was enlarged until it was brought into connexion with practically all of the known sciences, botany, chemistry, zoology, mineralogy, anatomy and medicine. Colours, metals, stones, plants, drugs and animal life of all kinds were associated with the planets and placed under their tutelage. In the system that passes under the name of Ptolemy, Saturn is associated with grey, Jupiter with white, Mars with red, Venus with yellow, while Mercury, occupying a peculiar place in Greek as it did in Babylonian astrology (where it was at one time designated as *the* planet *par excellence*), was supposed to vary its colour according to changing circumstances. The sun was associated with gold, the moon with silver, Jupiter with electrum, Saturn with lead, Venus with copper, and so on, while the continued influence of astrological motives is to be seen in the association of quicksilver, upon its discovery at a comparatively late period, with Mercury, because of its changeable character as a solid and a liquid. In the same way stones were connected with both the planets and the months; plants, by diverse association of ideas, were connected with the planets, and animals likewise were placed under the guidance and protection of one or other of the heavenly bodies. By this curious process of combination the entire realm of the natural sciences was translated into the language of astrology with the single avowed purpose of seeing in all phenomena signs indicative of what the future had in store. The fate of the individual, as that feature of the future which had a supreme interest, led to the association of the planets with parts of the body. Here, too, we find various systems devised, in part representing the views of different schools, in part reflecting advancing conceptions regarding the functions of the organs in man and animals. In one system the seat of Mercury, representing divine intelligence as the source of all knowledge—a view that reverts to Babylonia where Nebo (corresponding to Mercury) was regarded as the divine power to whom all wisdom is due—was placed in the liver as the primeval seat of the soul, whereas in other systems this distinction was assigned to Jupiter or to Venus. Saturn, taking in Greek astrology the place at the head of the planets which among the Babylonians was accorded to Jupiter-Marduk, was given a place in the brain, which in later times was looked upon as the centre of soul-life; Venus, as the planet of the passion of love, was supposed to reign supreme over the genital organs, the belly and the lower limbs; Mars, as the violent planet, is associated with the bile, as well as with the blood and kidneys. Again, the right ear is associated with Saturn, the left ear with Mars, the right eye in the case of the male with the sun and the left eye with the moon, while in the case of the female it was just the reverse. From the planets the same association of ideas was applied to the constellations of the zodiac, which in later phases of astrology are placed on a par with the planets themselves, so far as their importance for the individual horoscope is concerned. The fate of the individual in this combination of planets with the zodiac was made dependent not merely upon the planet which happened to be rising at the time of birth or of conception, but also upon its local relationship to a special sign or to certain signs of the zodiac. The zodiac was regarded as the prototype of the human body, the different parts of which all had their corresponding section in the zodiac itself. The head was placed in the first sign of the zodiac—the Ram; and the feet in the last sign—the Fishes. Between these two extremes the other parts and organs of the body were distributed among the remaining signs of the zodiac, the neck being assigned to the Bull, the shoulders and arms to the Gemini (or twins), the breast to Cancer, the flanks to Leo, the bladder to Virgo, the buttocks to the Balance, the pubis to the Scorpion, the thighs to Sagittarius, the knees to Capricorn, and the limbs to Aquarius. Not content with this, we find the late Egyptian astrologers setting up a correspondence between the thirty-six *decani* recognized by them and the human body, which is thus divided into thirty-six parts; to each part a god was assigned as a controlling force. With human anatomy thus connected with the planets, with constellations, and with single stars, medicine became an integral part of astrology, or, as we might also put it, astrology became the handmaid of medicine. Diseases and disturbances of the ordinary functions of the organs were attributed to the influence of planets or explained as due to conditions observed in a constellation or in the position of a star; and an interesting survival of this bond between astrology and medicine is to be seen in the use up to the present time of the sign of Jupiter ♃, which still heads medicinal prescriptions, while, on the other hand, the influence of planetary lore appears in the assignment of the days of the week to the planets, beginning with Sunday, assigned to the sun, and ending with Saturday, the day of Saturn. Passing on into still later periods, Saturn's day was associated with the Jewish sabbath, Sunday with the Lord's Day, Tuesday with Tiw, the god of war, corresponding to Mars of the Romans and to the Nergal of the Babylonians. Wednesday was assigned to the planet Mercury, the equivalent of the Germanic god Woden; Thursday to Jupiter, the equivalent of Thor; and Friday to Friga, the goddess of love, who is represented by Venus among the Romans and among the Babylonians by Ishtar. Astrological considerations likewise already regulated in ancient Babylonia the distinction of lucky and unlucky days, which passing down to the Greeks and Romans (*dies fasti* and *nefasti*) found a striking expression in Hesiod's *Works and Days*. Among the Arabs similar associations of lucky and unlucky days directly connected with the influence of the planets prevailed through all times, Tuesday and Wednesday, for instance, being regarded as the days for blood-letting, because Tuesday was connected with Mars, the lord of war and blood, and Wednesday with Mercury, the planet of humours. Even in modern times travellers relate how, when an auspicious day has been proclaimed by the astrologers, the streets of Bagdad may be seen running with blood from the barbers' shops.

It is unnecessary here to give a detailed analysis of the methods of judicial astrology as an art, or directions for the casting of a horoscope, or "nativity," *i.e.* a map of the heavens at the hour of birth, showing, according to the Ephemeris, the position of the heavenly bodies, from which their influence may be deduced. Each of the twelve signs of the zodiac is credited with its own characteristics and influence, and is the controlling sign of its "house of life." The sign exactly rising at the moment of birth is called the ascendant. The benevolent or malignant influence of each planet, together with the sun and moon, is modified by the sign it inhabits at the nativity; thus Jupiter in one house may indicate riches, fame in another, beauty in another, and Saturn similarly poverty, obscurity or deformity. The calculation is affected by the "aspects," *i.e.* according as the planets are near or far as regards one another (in conjunction, in semi-sextile, semi-square, sextile, quintile, square, trine, sesqui-quadrate, bi-quintile, opposition or parallel acclination). Disastrous signs predominate over auspicious, and the various effects are combined in a very elaborate and complicated manner.

Judicial astrology, as a form of divination, is a concomitant of natural astrology, in its purer astronomical aspect, but mingled with what is now considered an unscientific and superstitious view of world-forces. In the *Janua aurea reserata quatuor linguarum* (1643) of J. A. Comenius we find the following definition:—"*Astronomus siderum meatus seu motus considerat: Astrologus eorundem efficaciam, influxum, et effectum.*" Kepler was more cautious in his opinion; he spoke of astronomy as the wise mother, and astrology as the foolish daughter, but he added that the existence of the daughter was necessary to the life of the mother. Tycho Brahe and Gassendi both began with astrology, and it was only after pursuing the false science, and finding it wanting, that Gassendi devoted himself to astronomy. In their numerous allusions to the subtle mercury, which the one makes when treating of a means of measuring time by the efflux of the metal, and the other in a treatise on the transit of the planet, we see traces of the school in which they served their first apprenticeship. Huygens, moreover, in his great posthumous work, *Cosmotheoros, seu de terris coelestibus*, shows himself a more exact observer of astrological symbols than Kircher himself in his *Iter exstaticum*. Huygens contends that between the inhabitants of different planets there need not be any greater difference than exists between men of different types on the earth. "There are on the earth," continues this rational interpreter of the astrologers and chiromancers, "men of cold temperament who would thrive in Saturn, which is the farthest planet from the sun, and there are other spirits warm and ardent enough to live in Venus."

Those were indeed strange times, according to modern ideas, when astrologers were dominant by the terror they inspired, and sometimes by the martydom they endured when their predictions were either too true or too false. Faith, to borrow their own language, was banished to Virgo, and rarely shed her influence on men. Cardan (1501–1576), for instance, hated Luther, and so changed his birthday in order to give him an unfavourable horoscope. In Cardan's times, as in those of Augustus, it was a common practice for men to conceal the day and hour of their birth, till, like Augustus, they found a complaisant astrologer. But, as a general rule, medieval and Renaissance astrologers did not give themselves the trouble of reading the stars, but contented themselves with telling fortunes by faces. They practised chiromancy, and relied on afterwards drawing a horoscope to suit. As physiognomists their talent was undoubted, and according to Vanini there was no need to mount to the house-top to cast a nativity. "Yes," he says, "I can read his face; by his hair and his forehead it is easy to guess that the sun at his birth was in the sign of Libra and near Venus. Nay, his complexion shows that Venus touches Libra. By the rules of astrology he could not lie."

A few salient facts may be added concerning the astrologers and their predictions, remarkable either for their fulfilment or for the ruin and confusion they brought upon their authors. We may begin with one taken from Bacon's *Essay of Prophecies*:—
"When I was in France, I heard from one Dr Pena, that the queen mother, who was given to curious arts, caused the king her husband's nativitie to be calculated, under a false name; and the astrologer gave a judgment, that he should be killed in a duell; at which the queene laughed, thinking her husband to be above

challenges and duels; but he was slaine, upon a course at tilt, the splinters of the staffe of Mongomery going in at his bever." A favourite topic of the astrologers of all countries has been the immediate end of the world. As early as 1186 the earth had escaped one threatened cataclysm of the astrologers. This did not prevent Stöffler from predicting a universal deluge for the year 1524—a year, as it turned out, distinguished for drought. His aspect of the heavens told him that in that year three planets would meet in the aqueous sign of Pisces. The prediction was believed far and wide, and President Aurial, at Toulouse, built himself a Noah's ark—a curious realization, in fact, of Chaucer's merry invention in the *Miller's Tale.*

Tycho Brahe was from his fifteenth year devoted to astrology, and adjoining his observatory at Uranienburg the astronomer-royal of Denmark had a laboratory built in order to study alchemy, and it was only a few years before his death that he finally abandoned astrology. We may here notice one very remarkable prediction of the master of Kepler. That he had carefully studied the comet of 1577 as an astronomer, we may gather from his adducing the very small parallax of this comet as disproving the assertion of the Aristotelians that a solid sphere enveloped the heavens. But besides this, we find him in his character of astrologer drawing a singular prediction from the appearance of this comet. It announced, he tells us, that in the north, in Finland, there should be born a prince who should lay waste Germany and vanish in 1632. Gustavus Adolphus, it is well known, was born in Finland, overran Germany, and died in 1632. The fulfilment of the details of this prophecy suggests that Tycho Brahe had some basis of reason for his prediction. Born in Denmark of a noble Swedish family, a politician, as were all his contemporaries of distinction, Tycho, though no conjuror, could foresee the advent of some great northern hero. Moreover, he was doubtless well acquainted with a very ancient tradition, that heroes generally came from the northern frontiers of their native land, where they are hardened and tempered by the threefold struggle they wage with soil, climate and barbarian neighbours.

Kepler explained the double movement of the earth by the rotation of the sun. At one time the sun presented its friendly side, which attracted one planet, sometimes its adverse side, which repelled it. He also peopled the planets with souls and genii. He was led to his three great laws by musical analogies, just as William Herschel afterwards passed from music to astronomy. Kepler, who in his youth made almanacs, and once prophesied a hard winter, which came to pass, could not help putting an astrological interpretation on the disappearance of the brilliant star of 1572, which Tycho had observed. Theodore Beza thought that this star, which in December 1573 equalled Jupiter in brilliancy, predicted the second coming of Christ. Astronomers were only then beginning to study variable and periodic stars, and disturbances in that part of the heavens, which had till then, on the authority of Aristotle, been regarded as incorruptible, combined with the troubles of the times, must have given a new stimulus to belief in the signs in heaven. Montaigne (*Essais*, lib. i. chap, x.) relates a singular episode in the history of astrology. Charles V. and Francis I., who both bid for the friendship of the infamous Aretino, surnamed the divine, both likewise engaged astrologers to fight their battles. In Italy those who prophesied the ruin of France were sure to be listened to. These prophecies affected the public funds much as telegrams do nowadays. "At Rome," Montaigne tells us, "a large sum of money was lost on the Change by this prognostication of our ruin." The marquis of Saluces, notwithstanding his gratitude to Francis I. for the many favours he had received, including his marquisate, of which the brother was despoiled for his benefit, was led in 1536 to betray his country, being scared by the glorious prophecies of the ultimate success of Charles V. which were then rife. The influence of the Medici made astrologers popular in France. Richelieu, on whose council was Jacques Gaffarel (1601–1681), the last of the Kabbalists, did not despise astrology as an engine of government. At the birth of Louis XIV. a certain Morin de

Villefranche was placed behind a curtain to cast the nativity of the future autocrat. A generation back the astrologer would not have been hidden behind a curtain, but have taken precedence of the doctor. La Bruyère dares not pronounce against such beliefs, "for there are perplexing facts affirmed by grave men who were eye-witnesses." In England William Lilly and Robert Fludd were both dressed in a little brief authority. The latter gives us elaborate rules for the detection of a thief, and tells us that he has had personal experience of their efficacy. "If the lord of the sixth house is found in the second house, or in company with the lord of the second house, the thief is one of the family. If Mercury is in the sign of the Scorpion he will be bald, &c." Francis Bacon abuses the astrologers of his day no less than the alchemists, but he does so because he has visions of a reformed astrology and a reformed alchemy. Sir Thomas Browne, too, while he denies the capacity of the astrologers of his day, does not venture to dispute the reality of the science. The idea of the souls of men passing at death to the stars, the blessedness of their particular sphere being assigned them according to their deserts (the metempsychosis of J. Reynaud), may be regarded as a survival of religious astrology, which, even as late as Descartes's day, assigned to the angels the task of moving the planets and the stars. Joseph de Maistre believed in comets as messengers of divine justice, and in animated planets, and declared that divination by astrology is not an absolutely chimerical science. Lastly, we may mention a few distinguished men who ran counter to their age in denying stellar influences. Aristarchus of Samos, Martianus Capella (the precursor of Copernicus), Cicero, Favorinus, Sextus Empiricus, Juvenal, and in a later age Savonarola and Pico della Mirandola, and La Fontaine, a contemporary of the neutral La Bruyère, were all pronounced opponents of astrology.

In England Swift may fairly claim the credit of having given the death-blow to astrology by his famous squib, entitled *Prediction for the Year 1708, by Isaac Bickerstaff, Esq.* He begins, by professing profound belief in the art, and next points out the vagueness and the absurdities of the philomaths. He then, in the happiest vein of parody, proceeds to show them a more excellent way:—"My first prediction is but a trifle, yet I mention it to show how ignorant these sottish pretenders to astrology are in their own concerns: it refers to Partridge the almanac-maker. I have consulted the star of his nativity by my own rules, and find he will infallibly die upon the 29th of March next about eleven at night of a raging fever. Therefore I advise him to consider of it and settle his affairs in time." Then followed a letter to a person of quality giving a full and particular account of the death of Partridge on the very day and nearly at the hour mentioned. In vain the wretched astrologer protested that he was alive, got a literary friend to write a pamphlet to prove it, and published his almanac for 1709. Swift, in his reply, abused him for his want of manners in giving a gentleman the lie, answered his arguments *seriatim*, and declared that the evidence of the publication of another almanac was wholly irrelevant, "for Gadbury, Poor Robin, Dove and Way do yearly publish their almanacs, though several of them have been dead since before the Revolution." Nevertheless a field is found even to this day for almanacs of a similar type, and for popular belief in them.

To astrological politics we owe the theory of heaven-sent rulers, instruments in the hands of Providence, and saviours of society. Napoleon, as well as Wallenstein, believed in his star. Many passages in the older English poets are unintelligible without some knowledge of astrology. Chaucer wrote a treatise on the astrolabe; Milton constantly refers to planetary influences; in Shakespeare's *King Lear*, Gloucester and Edmund represent respectively the old and the new faith. We still *contemplate* and *consider*; we still speak of men as *jovial, saturnine* or *mercurial*; we still talk of the *ascendancy* of genius, or a *disastrous* defeat. In French *heur, malheur, heureux, malheureux*, are all derived from the Latin *augurium*; the expression *né sous une mauvaise étoile*, born under an evil star, corresponds (with the change of *étoile* into *astre*) to the word *malôtru*, in Provençal *malastrue*;

and *son étoile pâlit*, his star grows pale, belongs to the same class of illusions. The Latia *ex augurio* appears in the Italian *sciagura, sciagurato,* softened into *sciaura, sciaurato,* wretchedness, wretched. The influence of a particular planet has also left traces in various languages; but the French and English *jovial* and the English *saturnine* correspond rather to the gods who served as types in chiromancy than to the planets which bear the same names. In the case of the expressions *bien* or *mal luné*, well or ill mooned, *avoir un quartier de lune dans la tetê*, to have the quarter of the moon in one's head, the German *mondsüchtig* and the English *moonstruck* or *lunatic,* the fundamental idea lies in the strange opinions formerly held about the moon.

A CHAPTER FROM
1911 *Encyclopædia Britannica, Volume* 2

PREFACE

I HAVE pleasure in presenting this little book to students in the Science of Astrology, with the hope that they will find it useful, instructive, and simple.

It is not *perfect*, far from it; I, myself, am not perfect, but make as many, or perhaps more, mistakes than many people; but there it is, if you study it carefully, you will need no other book to instruct you in that branch of Astrology, for I have taken especial care that it should contain all the essential information necessary for the practice of Horary Astrology. *Horary* Astrology, unlike its sister *Genethliacal*, contains many stereotyped rules, to which there is but *one* interpretation: rules which mean *such a thing*, and *only* that thing ; the volume, therefore, does not possess that *originality* which characterises the " Guides." What I have aimed at principally is, to *amend, correct*, and simplify the rules as much as possible. Many of the writers on this subject are far *too* copious, they give so many different rules, positions, and contingencies, that the young student is utterly bewildered. I have tried to avoid this, but whether successfully or not the student alone must judge, for rules which are clear to me may be like Greek to him.

Now for a word of advice. Do not go into Part II before you understand Part I ; if you do, you will be baffled and confused at every step. The true *Key* to *Horary* Astrology is contained in Chapters X, XI, and XIV of Part I ; if you master these chapters properly, your course will be clear ; if not, you will be unable to judge *accurately* anything.

I have not given any examples of the mode of judgment, because I consider them worse than useless and *misleading* in this branch of the science.

I cannot impress too much upon the reader the necessity of avoiding setting figures for frivolous occasions. *Horary* Astrology is only reliable in cases of moment, and when the mind is perplexed and anxious, *then* a figure set will be *radical* and *clear* ; but to set a figure for any little trivial thing means disappointment, for you will find that it has neither head nor tail.

Edwin Raphael.

London, 1883.

TABLE OF CONTENTS

CONTENTS

CONTENTS

CONTENTS

CHAPTER IX   PAGE

CHAPTER X

Raphael's Horary Astrology

PART I

CHAPTER I

THE SYMBOLS EXPLAINED

LEARN, practise, and understand the following :—
That the planets are eight in number, and are thus
named and symbolised : ♅ Herschel, or Uranus ;
♄ Saturn ; ♃ Jupiter ; ♂ Mars ; ☉ the Sun ;
♀ Venus ; ☿ Mercury ; ☽ the Moon. Some astrologers
include ♆ Neptune, but we have nothing clear or
definite as to his power, which at the best can effect but
little, owing to his immense distance from our earth.

The signs are as follow :—

Northern	♈ Aries	Southern	♎ Libra
	♉ Taurus		♏ Scorpio
	♊ Gemini		♐ Sagittarius
	♋ Cancer		♑ Capricorn
	♌ Leo		♒ Aquarius
	♍ Virgo		♓ Pisces

Each sign contains 30°, which, multiplied by the
twelve signs, give 360°, being the total number of
degrees contained in the Zodiac.

The Planetary Aspects

⌄ Semisextile	△ Trine
∠ Semisquare	⧄ Sesquiquadrate
✳ Sextile	☍ Opposition
☐ Square	P Parallel

There is also the position, ☌ Conjunction.

Of the Natures of the Aspects

The ☌ Conjunction is when two planets have the
same geocentric longitude. This aspect is found to
be good with good planets, but evil with evil planets ;
its effects are strong in all cases.

1

The ⌄ Semisextile is always good.
The ∠ Semisquare is always evil.
The ✳ Sextile is always good.
The ☐ Square is always evil.
The △ Trine is always good.
The ⬓ Sesquiquadrate is always evil.
The ☍ Opposition is always evil.
The P Parallel, this is like the ☌ both in effect
and nature.

*Of the Natures and Qualities of the Signs of the
Zodiac*

The signs are classified and divided as follow :—

Masculine Signs—♈ ♊ ♌ ♎ ♐ ♒.

Feminine Signs— ♉ ♋ ♍ ♏ ♑ ♓.

Fiery Signs—♈ ♌ ♐ ; *earthy*— ♉ ♍ ♑ ; *airy*—
♊ ♎ ♒ ; *watery*—♋ ♏ ♓.

Signs of *Short* Ascension—♑ ♒ ♓ ♈ ♉ ♊.

Signs of *Long* Ascension—♋ ♌ ♍ ♎ ♏ ♐.

Moveable and *Cardinal* Signs—♈ ♋ ♎ ♑.

Fixed Signs— ♉ ♌ ♏ ♒.

Common Signs—♊ ♍ ♐ ♓.

Fruitful Signs—♋ ♏ ♓.

Barren Signs—♊ ♌ and ♍.

Double-bodied Signs—♊ ♓ and the first half ♐ .

Equinoctial Signs—♈ and ♎.

Tropical Signs—♋ and ♑.

*Study well these divisions, as they are very important,
and must not be overlooked.*

CHAPTER II

CONCERNING THE MEASUREMENT OF THE PLANETARY ASPECTS

THE whole Zodiac contains 360 degrees, or twelve
signs of 30 degrees each.   The signs run in order thus,
and remain so always :—

♈ ♉ ♊ ♋ ♌ ♍ ♎ ♏ ♐ ♑ ♒ ♓.

Now from ♈ 0° to ♉ 0° is 30°; from ♈ 0° to ♊ 0° is 60°; or from ♈ 15° to ♊ 15° is 60°; from ♉ 0° to ♍ 0° is 120°; or from ♑ 0° to ♉ 0° is 120°—being four signs apart, and so on with the other signs in like way.

The first aspect (this, properly speaking, is a " position ") we take will be the ☌ conjunction, which is when two or more planets are in the same sign, degree, and minute.

The second aspect is the ⚺ (semisextile), or 1 sign, or 30° distant. Thus :—♂ in ♉ 5°, and ♄ in ♊ 5° will be 30°, or 1 sign apart.

The third aspect is the ∠ (semisquare), or 45°, or 1½ signs apart. Thus :—♀ in ♉, 15°, and ♃ in ♋, 0°, will be 45°, or 1½ signs apart; for, from ♉ 15° to the end of ♉ will be 15°, and ♊ contains 30°, then 15° + 30° = 45°, as ♋ 0° is at the end of ♊. *Observe this example with all the other aspects.*

The fourth aspect is the ✳ (sextile), or 2 signs, or 60° apart. Thus :—♂ in ♎, 4°; and ♃ in ♐, 4°— will be 2 signs or 60° apart.

The fifth is the ☐, or 3 signs, or 90° apart.

The sixth is the △, or 4 signs, or 120° apart.

The seventh is the ⛢, or 4½ signs, or 135° apart.

The eighth is the ☍, or 6 signs, or 180° apart.

The ninth is the P, or an equal distance in declination, either north or south from the equator.

The planets cannot be more than 180° apart, and they are then in opposition, after which the distance between them decreases.

NOTE.—The fiery signs are in trine aspect to each other. Thus ♈ is in △ to ♌ and ♐, and ♌ is in △ to ♈ and ♐, and ♐ is in △ to ♈ and ♌. The same is the case with the earthy, airy, and watery signs. The common, cardinal, or moveable and fixed signs are in ☐ and ☍ to each other, thus—♉ is in ☐ to ♌, and in ☍ to ♏, and so on with the others.

THE ORBS OF THE PLANETS

These are the number of degrees in which one planet operates with another. The orb of ♅ is 8° ; ♄, 8° ; ♃, 10° ; ♂, 8° ; ☉, 17° ; ♀, 8° ; ☿, 8° ; ☽, 12°. They are generally determined thus : if two planets are approaching a ☌, or aspect, add the orbs of the two planets together, and divide by two ; and when the planets get within that number of degrees, they begin to exert an influence jointly. For example, suppose the Sun is approaching the ☌ of ♂, you add their two orbs together, which is 25°, and divide by two, which is 12½° ; therefore, when the ☉ gets within 12½° of ♂, the effects of the ☉ ☌ ♂ commence. It is the same with the other planets.

CHAPTER III

DESCRIPTIONS OF PERSONS PRODUCED BY THE PLANETS IN THE TWELVE SIGNS

Herschel

♅ in *Aries* denotes a rather tall person, lean and well made, light brown hair, grey eyes, ruddy in complexion, strong constitution, inquisitive, fond of science, inventive, and ambitious.

♅ in *Taurus*.—Rather short stature, dark hair and eyes, dull complexion, thick set, strong, conceited, boasting, secret, and a great eater.

♅ in *Gemini*.—Tall, thin stature, light brown hair and grey eyes, quick step, very active, fond of science, good in disposition, and eccentric.

♅ in *Cancer*.—A short, thick set person, stout, pale in complexion, dark brown hair, conceited, and very fond of drink and women.

♅ in *Leo*.—Large stature, broad, strong shoulders, light brown hair, sandy whiskers, firm walk, ambitious, generous, independent, and determined.

♅ in *Virgo*.—Rather short stature, dark hair and

eyes, lean body, small limbs, very eccentric, independent, and ingenious ; secret and close.

♅ in *Libra*.—Well-made, strong body, round face, light hair, sanguine complexion ; one who delights in science, learning, and literature, quick in anger, and independent.

♅ in *Scorpio*.—Short thick-set body, broad shoulders, ill-made hands, swarthy complexion, black hair and eyes ; very malicious and deceitful, fond of drink, women, and pleasure.

♅ in *Sagittary*.—Tall upright person, high forehead, light brown hair and eyes, good complexion ; very fond of sports ; generous and ambitious.

♅ in *Capricorn*.—Middle stature, short neck, yet well made, high forehead, light brown hair, and small dark eyes ; proud, austere, and conceited, and not to be trusted.

♅ in *Aquarius*.—Middle stature, brown hair and eyes, handsome, round face ; very ingenious, fond of novelties, and very independent and eccentric.

♅ in *Pisces*.—Short stature, pale in complexion, dark hair and eyes, fleshy, ill-formed feet and legs ; fond of drink, females, and gluttony.

Saturn

♄ in *Aries* represents one of a moderate stature, ruddy complexion, but somewhat obscure, high forehead, great full eyes, dark hair, but little beard ; a spare, lean person ; a great boaster of his actions ; an ill-natured, quarrelsome, contentious person.

♄ in *Taurus*.—He represents one of a mean stature, a lean body, a heavy lumpish person, dark hair, and uncomely look ; he is generally inclined to vicious and sordid actions, and delights in all sorts of dissipation and venereal pursuits.

♄ in *Gemini*.—He represents one of an indifferent, tall stature, an oval visage, the hair black or brownish, a well-proportioned body, humane, and ingenious, but of a perverse nature and disposition.

♄ in *Cancer*.—He signifies one of an indifferent stature, of a sickly constitution of body, thin face, and brownish hair ; sometimes the person is crooked, ill-shaped, and ill-conditioned, inclined to malice and hatred ; viciously inclined, and often a drunkard.

♄ in *Leo*.—He represents one tall, big-boned, not very much inclined to fatness, the hair of a light brown ; his temper and disposition tolerably good, but somewhat passionate and malicious ; he appears honest, but is not to be trusted.

♄ in *Virgo*.—He signifies a tall, spare body, swarthy complexion, brown or black hair ; a melancholy person, somewhat inclined to study, malicious, and, when angry, will be long before he is pleased again ; he is inclined to theft, and a person of reserved thoughts, and generally in an unfortunate condition,

♄ in *Libra*.—He represents a person of large stature, a well composed body, oval visage, a large forehead, and brown hair ; he is high spirited, very much conceited in his own actions, somewhat prodigal and expensive, and soon moved to anger ; inclined to controversy, and often victor.

♄ in *Scorpio*.—He signifies a person of a low stature, broad shoulders, and brown or black hair ; he is quarrelsome, much given to debate and contentions, and all sordid actions.

♄ in *Sagittary*.—He represents a well composed person of an indifferent large stature, brown hair, courteous in his behaviour to all persons, but will not take any provocation ; he is choleric, but soon reconciled, and merciful.

♄ in *Capricorn*.—He represents one of a middle stature, not very tall, a lean, spare person, long visage, little eyes, brown or black hair, an obscure, sallow complexion ; he is covetous of worldly goods, a melancholy person, using but few words ; he is peevish, and will retain anger a long time.

♄ in *Aquarius*.—He gives a middle stature, brown

or black hair, rather inclined to stoutness than otherwise ; he is of a courteous disposition, an ingenious fancy, a lover of arts, yet conceited of his own ingenuity.

♄ in *Pisces*.—He signifies one of a middle stature, of a pale complexion, black or brown hair, full eyes, and a great head ; an ill-conditioned, malicious, contentious, dissembling person, very fond of drink.

⁎ *Persons signified by Saturn are rarely, if ever, to be trusted. They have much deceit, are nervous, and awkward.*

Jupiter

♃ in *Aries* denotes one of a middle stature, of a ruddy complexion, an oval visage, the hair of a brown or flaxen colour, a quick piercing eye ; a very obliging person, of a free and noble disposition, a lover of friendship, peace, and tranquillity.

♃ in *Taurus*.—He represents one of a mean stature, not well formed, complexion swarthy, the hair brown ; his condition is good ; a lover of women, yet of a good carriage ; a wise, discreet person, and humane.

♃ in *Gemini*.—He denotes a large, tall person, something above the middle stature, brown hair, and a well composed body ; courteous in his behaviour, and obliging to all persons ; he delights in women's company, and is a lover of arts and sciences.

♃ in *Cancer*.—He signifies a person of middle stature, a pale sickly complexion, and oval visage ; he has dark brown or black hair ; is a very pleasant person ; he hath aspiring thoughts, and aims at great things ; a busy body, that loves to concern himself with other men's affairs, and a great lover of females.

♃ in *Leo*.—He represents one of a tall stature, and of a well composed body ; light coloured hair, or sometimes yellow and curling ; comely eyes, of a ruddy complexion, and good disposition ; bold and stout-hearted, delighting in manly and valiant actions, and very desirous of honour.

♃ in *Virgo*.—He signifies a well composed person,

with black or brown hair ; he is much given to the study of arts and sciences, of a choleric disposition, and covetous, ambitious of honour, and a lover of money, and generally handsome.

♃ in *Libra*.—He represents a person of a neat, well composed body, of a pleasant countenance, an oval visage, light brown or flaxen hair ; of a very good disposition, delighting in all pleasant exercises and recreations, and by his good behaviour he is beloved of all men, and is very obliging and courteous.

♃ in *Scorpio*.—He denotes one of a middle stature, rather inclined to be stout, of a dusky complexion, brownish hair ; he is conceited and close in nature, covetous of worldly goods, and thinks himself above his equals.

♃ in *Sagittary*.—He represents one of a tall stature, a ruddy complexion, an oval visage, the hair of a chestnut colour ; a well composed person, of very good behaviour, just in his actions, a lover of horses, and a good horseman.

♃ in *Capricorn*.—He signifies one of a very little stature, thin face, pale complexion, and brown hair ; a very weakly person, peevish, sickly, and ill-natured.

♃ in *Aquarius*.—He signifies a person of middle stature, good complexion, brown hair, and a well-set person, of a pleasant, merry disposition, delighting in good company, and very just in his actions.

♃ in *Pisces*.—He represents one of a mean stature, but inclined to be stout, the hair of a light brown ; he is a lover of mirth and musical instruments, is studious in several arts and sciences, very ingenious, delighting in good company and pleasant recreations, and fortunate by water.

Mars

♂ in *Aries* signifies one of middle stature, big-boned, and a well-set person, of a swarthy complexion ; sometimes the hair is red, or of a light colour and curling, a sharp hazel eye ; of a bold, confident countenance, ambitious of rule, a lover of war and contests.

♂ in *Taurus*.—He represents one of a middle stature, but not tall, a dull complexion, a broad face, a great wide mouth, black hair, and no very pleasant person ; he has often a wound or scar on the face ; he signifies a treacherous, false, dissembling person ; gluttonous, luxurious, and a lover of lewd women's company.

♂ in *Gemini*.—He denotes one of a tall stature, a well proportioned body, hair black, or brown, of a wandering, unsettled mind, choleric disposition, and a rash, turbulent spirit.

♂ in *Cancer*.—He describes a person of a short stature, disproportioned body, sometimes deformed by crookedness, etc., the hair is brown, and the complexion is pale ; he signifies a sottish, dull-spirited person, a lover of wine, a promoter of quarrels, and a mean person.

♂ in *Leo*.—He represents one of a tall, strong, able body, his hair of a dark flaxen colour, a large face, and great eyes, a very hasty, choleric person, of a free-hearted, generous spirit, delighting in shooting and all warlike exercises.

♂ in *Virgo*.—He describes a well proportioned person of middle stature, of a swarthy complexion, brown or black hair ; soon angry, and long before he be pleased again ; a person very ill-conditioned, and unfortunate in most of his actions.

♂ in *Libra*.—He describes a person rather tall, and of well composed body, an oval visage, the hair of a light brown, sanguine complexion, and a pleasant, cheerful countenance ; a lover of women's company, and ambitious of his own praise.

♂ in *Scorpio*.—He represents one of a middle stature, a swarthy complexion, broad face, black hair and curling ; an ungrateful, revengeful, quarrelsome person, but yet very ingenious in several arts and sciences.

♂ in *Sagittarius*.—He describes one of a tall stature, and in every part well proportioned, an oval visage, brown hair, and very good complexion ; he delights in good merry company, he is of choleric disposition, delighting in war and warlike exercises.

♂ in *Capricorn*.—He represents one of a mean stature, lean body, thin face, little head, and black hair, but an indifferent complexion ; of a good spirit, ingenious and quick-witted, good disposition, and fortunate in his actions.

♂ in *Aquarius*.—He represents one of a middle stature, a well proportioned body, a good complexion, the hair red, or sandy and flaxen ; he is very quarrelsome, and much given to controversy, which many times proves to his own prejudice.

♂ in *Pisces*.—He describes one of a short stature, but fleshy, the hair of a light brown or flaxen colour, the body not very handsomely composed ; he delights in the company of lewd women, is very dissembling, and of a dull and stupid understanding.

Sun

☉ in *Aries* represents one of a middle stature, strong and well composed body, good complexion, the hair of a light flaxen or golden colour ; he is of a noble disposition, delighting in war ; he is a terror to his enemies, gaining much honour and renown therein.

☉ in *Taurus*.—He describes a well set person, of a short stature, but not very comely, a broad face, wide mouth, great nose, dull complexion, brown hair, a bold, confident person, delighting in war, and is often victorious.

☉ in *Gemini*.—He describes one of a large stature, of a sanguine complexion, brown hair, and a well composed body ; he is courteous in his actions, and of a good disposition, yet not very fortunate in his affairs, but yet content, and will pass by slight abuses.

☉ in *Cancer*.—He denotes one of little stature, of an unhealthful disposition of body, an ill complexion with some defects in the face, he has brown hair, and is a good-natured person, of a pleasant disposition, delighting in merry company, sports, and pastimes ; he is a lover of women's company, and a free humoured, jovial person.

⊙ in *Leo.*—He represents a strong well proportioned person ; he has a full face, large eyes, light or yellow hair, a sanguine complexion ; he is faithful and just to his friends, and courteous to all men ; he performs his promises fully, and is desirous of honour ; he has sometimes a scar in his face ; he delights in good pleasant company.

⊙ in *Virgo.*—He represents a well proportioned body, but of a very large stature, not very stout ; the hair of a brown or black, and much of it ; he is of good complexion, and a good disposition ; one that delights in all civil recreations, and a very pleasant ingenious person.

⊙ in *Libra.*—He describes one of an upright straight body, a good complexion, an oval visage, a full eye, bright coloured hair, unfortunate in his actions, especially in warlike affairs, he loses his honour, and is much exposed to danger.

⊙ in *Scorpio.*—He represents one of a middle stature, well set person, dull complexion ; he has a full, fleshy face, and brown hair, the whole body inclined to be stout ; he is of a rugged nature, but very ingenious, and desirous of honour ; he is expert in war, also in physic and chemistry, and fortunate on the sea.

⊙ in *Sagittarius.*—He describes a comely tall, well composed person, of a sanguine complexion, an oval visage, the hair of a light brown ; a high spirited, proud person, ambitious of honour, delighting in war ; he is active and pleasant, and scorns to take advantage of any.

⊙ in *Capricorn.*—He describes one of little stature, of a pale complexion, a lean spare body, not very well proportioned, an oval visage, and brown hair ; he is of a good disposition, very ingenious, and victorious in war ; he is of an undaunted spirit, and delights in women's company.

⊙ in *Aquarius.*—He represents one of a well composed, corpulent body, of middle stature, a good complexion, of a full round face, and light brown hair, and desirous of bearing rule over others.

⊙ in *Pisces.*—He describes a person of a low stature, a tolerably good complexion, a round face, light brown or flaxen hair ; a corpulent body ; he delights in merriments, and in keeping women's company, in sports and games ; he is expensive and prodigal !

Venus

♀ in *Aries* represents a slender body of a middle stature, of a good complexion, light hair, and an indifferent well proportioned body, but very unfortunate in his actions ; he is sometimes a lover of company and very extravagant.

♀ in *Taurus.*—She represents one of a middle stature, a comely, well proportioned person, of a good complexion, dark brown hair ; one of a very good disposition, for which he is beloved of every one ; he is fortunate in his actions, and obliging to all persons.

♀ in *Gemini.*—She represents a slender, tall, well proportioned person, brown hair, and of a good complexion ; he is loving and free-hearted, and hates all unjust actions ; he is merciful and charitable to the poor, and honest in all his actions.

♀ in *Cancer.*—She describes one of a short stature, a body rather inclined to fatness, a pale complexion, round face, light coloured hair ; he is mutable and inconstant ; is gluttonous, idle, a lover of good company, and vain recreations.

♀ in *Leo.*—She represents one of a moderately tall stature, and a well proportioned body, good complexion, round face, full eye, the hair of a light brown or sandy flaxen, sometimes freckles in the face ; his conditions are indifferently good ; he is passionate, but his anger is soon over ; he is generous, free, and rather proud.

♀ in *Virgo*.—She describes one moderately tall, of a well composed body, an obscure complexion, oval visage, and dark brown or black hair ; a very ingenious person, but often crossed in his understanding ; he is an active, subtle person, and of a very searching fancy.

♀ in *Libra*.—She describes a well proportioned, tall upright person, of a sanguine complexion, an oval visage, and dimples in the cheeks, sometimes freckles in the face, with comely brown hair ; a courteous, civil, respectable person, who delights in good and virtuous company.

♀ in *Scorpio*.—She represents one of a middle stature, and a well set person, somewhat stout ; a broad face, dark brown or black hair, a dull complexion ; she denotes a quarrelsome person, hateful, envious, a lover of contentious and unworthy actions.

♀ in *Sagittary*.—She represents one of a tall stature, a clear complexion, an oval visage, light brown hair, and a well composed person, of a good disposition, of a noble spirit, delighting in pleasant recreations, but a little proud and passionate, yet he will not continue long in anger.

♀ in *Capricorn*.—She describes one of middle stature, a lean, spare person, of a sickly complexion, thin face, dark brown or black hair ; a lover of women ; he is much given to drinking, and talking of his pleasure, but not very fortunate in his actions.

♀ in *Aquarius*.—She describes a handsome, decent, well composed body, a very good complexion, the hair of a light brown or flaxen colour ; a person of a very good disposition, very courteous and obliging to all men, and a hater of evil actions, a lover of peace and quietness, and takes delight in recreation.

♀ in *Pisces*.—She denotes a person of middle stature, of a good complexion, a round face, sometimes a dimple in the chin, the hair of a light brown or flaxen colour, and one of a very good disposition ; he has an ingenious wit, is just in his actions, and a lover of peace and tranquillity.

Mercury

☿ in *Aries* describes one of a short stature ; a lean, spare body, an oval visage, no clear complexion, light brown hair ; a quarrelsome, discontented person ; giving to lying, theft, and breeding of strife and contentions.

☿ in *Taurus*.—He represents one of a middle stature, a well set, corpulent body, swarthy complexion, and dark brown hair ; he is a great lover of company, and of women ; he is a slothful person, and one that loves his own ease.

☿ in *Gemini*.—He describes a well composed body, reasonably tall of stature, of a good complexion, the hair of a light brown ; he represents a very ingenious person, a lover of arts and sciences, who will easily attain them without a teacher.

☿ in *Cancer*.—He represents a person of mean stature, of an ill complexion, a thin face, sharp nose, little eyes, dark brown hair ; a malicious, knavish, sottish person ; given to lying, stealing, and dissimulation.

☿ in *Leo*.—He describes one of large stature, of a swarthy complexion, a round face, large eyes, and light brown hair ; a choleric, proud person, delighting in quarrels and contention, and a lover of mischief.

☿ in *Virgo*.—He represents a tall, slender, well composed person, of an obscure complexion, a long visage, the hair of a brown or black ; but a person sufficiently ingenious, delighting in good apparel, according to the capacity of his birth and quality.

☿ in *Libra*.—He describes one of a moderately tall stature, a well proportioned body, of a sanguine complexion, the hair of a light brown ; a wise, ingenious person of a very good disposition, just in all his actions, and a hater of vices ; he is a lover of learning, and a virtuous person.

☿ in *Scorpio*.—He describes a person of a middle stature, and a well set, strong, able body ; a swarthy complexion, dark brown hair, and curling ; he is a great lover of company ; a lover of women, and of an ingenious wit.

☿ in *Sagittary*.—He describes one of a tall stature, a ruddy complexion, an oval visage, large nose, and brown hair ; he is quarrelsome and contentious, and thereby proves an enemy to himself.

☿ in *Capricorn*.—He represents one of a little stature, thin face and muddy complexion, light brown hair, sometimes bow-legged ; a sickly person, of a peevish disposition, and unfortunate in many of his actions.

☿ in *Aquarius*.—He describes a person of a middle stature, a corpulent fleshy body, a full face, brown hair, and of a good complexion ; he is very ingenious in several arts and sciences ; an obliging person, one that is well beloved of his friends.

☿ in *Pisces*.—He represents one of little stature, of a sickly, pale complexion, thin face, and brown hair ; one much given to drinking and to women's company, and he wastes much of his estate thereby.

Moon

☽ in *Aries* represents one of a middle stature, reasonably fleshy, a round face, light brown hair, and one of a good complexion ; of a choleric, churlish disposition ; ambitious of honour, but not very fortunate in his actions.

☽ in *Taurus*.—She describes one of a middle stature, and a well composed, strong, corpulent body, black or dark brown hair ; one of a good behaviour ; a sober, obliging person, and just in all his actions, whereby he sometimes obtains preferment, and is beloved of all men.

☽ in *Gemini*.—She represents a tall person, but very

well proportioned ; dark brown hair, and of a good complexion ; but one of an ill nature, crafty, and deceitful ; an ingenious and subtle person, but not very fortunate in his affairs.

☽ in *Cancer.*—She describes a well proportioned person of middle stature, inclined to fatness ; of a pale complexion, round face, and dark brown hair ; one of a good disposition, of a wise and prudent behaviour, just in his actions, and fortunate in all his affairs.

☽ in *Leo.*—She represents a well proportioned body, of a large stature, a sanguine complexion, a full face, large eyes, and light brown hair ; a proud, ambitious person, domineering over others, and hates to be under subjection to any, and beloved by few.

☽ in *Virgo.*—She describes a person of large stature, of an indifferent good complexion, an oval visage, the hair black or dark brown ; a covetous, pensive, and melancholy person ; ingenious, but unfortunate in his actions.

☽ in *Libra.*—She describes one moderately tall, of a well composed person, and sanguine complexion, the hair of a light brown ; a person of a very good dis-position, and delighting in all pleasant recreations—as music, dancing, etc. ; taking much pleasure in women's company.

☽ in *Scorpio.*—She represents one of a short stature, but oftentimes very fat, and of an obscure com-plexion ; black hair or of a dark brown ; and one of an ill disposition ; a malicious, treacherous, sottish person.

☽ in *Sagittary.*—She describes one of a middle stature, and a well proportioned person ; of a san-guine complexion, an oval visage, and light brown hair ; she signifies one a little choleric and hasty, but soon pleased again ; ambitious of honour, and a very obliging person.

☽ in *Capricorn.*—She represents one of a spare, lean body, and a little stature, brown or black hair, and often they have some little defect in the knees ; one given to drinking, and to women's company, and an idle person, delighting in no good exercises or amusements.

☽ in *Aquarius*.—She represents a person of middle stature, a well composed, corpulent body, a sanguine complexion, and brown hair ; he is of a a courteous disposition, and of an ingenious searching fancy, delighting in moderate recreations, and a hater of all evil actions, whereby he is beloved of all persons.

☽ in *Pisces*.—She represents one of a low stature, and pale complexion, the body somewhat inclined to stoutness, the hair of a light brown ; an idle person very fond of drink and pleasure.

The use of these descriptions is this—first, to show you if a figure be really radical, or proper to be judged, in which case the querent will answer to the description of the sign and planet that may be rising, or if no planet be rising he will answer the description of the sign. If his appearance does not agree with the sign ascending, then it is best not to give judgment, because the querent's state of mind is not sufficiently intent or fixed to allow a proper answer to be given to his questions.

Then again, suppose he inquires about his friends, enemies, servants, etc., the foregoing descriptions will enable you to describe them exactly, and point out them to him, and in this way especially will they be found useful.

CHAPTER IV

THE SIGNIFICATIONS OF THE PLANETS

Herschel

♅ is a cold, dry, masculine, malevolent planet, and represents one of middle stature, well and strongly made, small bones, especially in the lower part of the frame ; high forehead, dark hair, small sharp eyes,

3

small ears, thin beard, and a countenance marked
with much determination and independence ; he is
profound in judgment, contemplative, independent,
intolerable ; of much dignity and self-conceit,
caring nothing for friends or enemies, estranged from
parents and kindred, headstrong, and easily angered.
If badly aspected, then he shows one very depraved
and immoral, of a murderous mind, cruel, acute,
and ready for any kind of badness, and impulsive.
When well placed, fond of science, study, and learning,
and of curiosities and uncommon things.

He governs in a great measure the brain and the
organs of curiosity, wonder, and sublimity.

The *diseases* of ♅ are such as can rarely be cured ;
all complex diseases ; derangements of the stomach,
and wind.

Employment.—All uncommon employments, as
astrologers, mesmerisers, antiquarians, phrenologists,
chemists, sculptors, and metaphysicians.

Places.—Railway stations, asylums, steam engines,
gas houses, and all places where engines are made.

Saturn

♄ is cold, dry, melancholy, earthy, masculine,
solitary, malevolent, being the most malignant of
all the planets. He represents one of a middle
stature, of a dark or pale complexion; small black
leering eyes ; lowering brows ; thick nose and lips ;
large ears ; dark hair ; broad shoulders ; thin beard ;
small thighs and legs, and a melancholy expression.
If well dignified either by house or benevolent
aspect, the person signified by ♄ will be constant
both in attachment and hatred, acute, penetrating,
grave, sober, but austere, rigid, and covetous. If
ill dignified, the querent will be sordid, base, jealous
and envious ; a cowardly, dissembling, lying, malicious
person, and immoveably stubborn ; will see every-
thing in its worst light, which generates fear, suspicion,
distrust, and repining.

He governs the spleen, right ear, bones, and retentive faculties.

The *Diseases* ♄ indicates are all those proceeding from cold and obstructed perspiration, melancholy, epilepsy, black jaundice, leprosy, fistulas, pains in the limbs and joints, gout, deafness and insanity, rheumatism, nervousness, stammering and dumbness.

Employment.—Curriers, farmers, miners underground, tinners, potters, broom men, plumbers, brick makers, maltsters, chimney sweepers, sextons of churches, bearers of corpses, scavengers, hostlers, colliers, carters, gardeners, chandlers, dyers of black cloth, and herdsmen, shepherds, and cow-keepers.

Places.—He delights in deserts, woods, obscure valleys, caves, dens, holes, mountains, or where men have been buried, church-yards, ruinous buildings, coal mines, sinks, and all dirty and stinking places.

Jupiter

♃ is next to Saturn, and the most powerful planet in our system, yet of a far different tendency, being hot, moist, and sanguine. He describes one of an erect, tall, stature ; good complexion ; an oval countenance ; high forehead ; full grey or brown eyes ; thick brown hair ; a handsome yet robust person ; and if well dignified, of very engaging manners and disposition, magnanimous, just, and upright.

If ill dignified, the native will be hypocritical, profligate, licentious, dull, conceited, and, according to time and place, a sycophant or a tyrant, proud, haughty, and extravagant.

He rules the lungs, liver, veins, and blood ; also the digestive and natural faculties.

The *Diseases* under him are affections of the internal viscera, and all those complaints which originate through a plethoric habit and corrupt blood, pleurisies, apoplexies, infirmities in the back and arteries.

Employment.—He signifies judges, senators, counsellors, ecclesiastical men, bishops, priests, ministers, cardinals, chancellors, doctors of the civil law, young scholars and students in a university or college, lawyers, clothiers, and woollen drapers.

Places.—He delights in being near altars of churches, in public conventions, synods, convocations, wardrobes, courts of justice, and oratories.

Mars

♂ is a hot, fiery, dry, masculine, and violent planet, and produces a person strong, well set, and, though of short stature, not fat, but muscular, with large bones ; the face brown or ruddy, round, and of bold expression ; red or light hair, and sharp hazel eyes. When well dignified, the person signified will be possessed of an active, bold, and intrepid mind, careless of danger, so that he may but triumph over his enemy ; yet magnanimous, and at the same time prudent in private concerns. But when ill dignified, either by position or an evil aspect of ♅ or ♄, then the querent is of a ferocious countenance, and wholly destitute of virtue ; prone to violence, treachery, robbery, murder, treason, and every species of cruelty and wickedness, fearing neither God nor man.

♂ rules the gall, the face, and left ear and hand, smell, and imagination.

The *Diseases* under him are fevers, plagues, and other inflammatory complaints ; jaundice, cutaneous eruptions, diabetes, strangury, burns, scalds, wounds, and bruises.

Qualities of Men and their Professions.— Generals of armies, colonels, captains, or persons having command in armies ; all kinds of soldiers, physicians, apothecaries, surgeons, chemists, gunners, butchers, marshals, sergeants, bailiffs, hangmen, thieves, smiths, bakers, armourers, watchmakers, cutlers of swords and knives, barbers, dyers, cooks, carpenters, gamesters, tanners, and curriers, according as ♂ may be strong or weak.

Places.—Smiths' shops, furnaces, slaughter houses, places where bricks or charcoal are burned, or have been burned, forges, battle-fields, and camps.

Sol, or the Sun

The ☉ is masculine, temperately hot and dry, and generally describes one of a large, bony, strong body; sallow complexion; large high forehead, shaded with light or sandy curling hair, which falls off at a comparatively early age; a fine, full piercing hazel eye, and the limbs straight and well proportioned.

If he is well dignified, the person will be noble, magnanimous, generous, humane, benevolent, affable; in friendship faithful and sincere, in promises slow but punctual, and often thoughtful, secret, and reserved; his gait is majestic; he is a lover of sumptuousness and magnificence, and superior to anything sordid, base, or dishonourable.

If ☉ be ill dignified, then will the querent be extravagant, loquacious, proud, arrogant, restless, troublesome, domineering; of no gravity; inclined to cruelty, mischief, and ill-nature; a sycophant to his superiors, at the same time disdaining them.

His *Diseases* are palpitations of the heart, fainting and swooning, weakness of sight, fevers, disorders of the brain, cramps, and disorders in the mouth and throat.

He is said to govern the heart, back, reins, right eye of man, and left eye of woman.

Employments.—He signifies kings, princes, emperors, etc., dukes, marquises, earls, barons, lieutenants, deputy lieutenants of counties, magistrates, gentlemen in general, courtiers, mayors, high sheriffs, high constables, stewards of noblemen's houses, the principal magistrate of any town, city, castle, or country village; goldsmiths, braziers, pewterers, coppersmiths, and masters generally.

Places.—Courts of princes, palaces, theatres, all

magnificent structures, being clean and decent, halls and dining rooms.

Venus

♀ is a feminine planet, cold and moist. She describes a handsome, well formed, but not tall person, a lovely blue eye, a handsome face, the hair of a light brown colour, and a sweet voice.

When well dignified, the querent will be of a quiet, engaging, sweet disposition; endowed with many accomplishments, amatory, fond of company and the society of the opposite sex, and a votary to pleasure.

If the planet be afflicted or ill dignified, then the person indicated will be riotous, profligate, regardless of credit or reputation, drunken, fond of loose company, and depraved in habits.

♀ rules the reins, spine, generative system, neck, throat, and breast.

The *Diseases* of Venus are seated in the back, loins, and the aforesaid parts; she also causes heartburn, palpitation, dislocation, and disorders arising from luxury and free living.

Employments.—Musicians, gamesters, silkmen, mercers, linen-drapers, painters, jewellers, players, lapidaries, embroiderers, woman-tailors, wives, mothers, virgins, choristers, fiddlers, pipers; when joined with the Moon, ballad-singers, perfumers, seamstresses, picture-drawers, engravers, upholsterers, glovers, and such as sell those commodities which adorn women, either in body or in face.

Mercury

☿ is cold, dry, and melancholy. He represents one of a tall, straight, thin body, narrow face, long nose, thin lips and chin; little beard, brown complexion, with hazel or chestnut hair, and the limbs and extremities long and slender.

This planet, well dignified, shows a strong, subtle imagination, incomparable understanding, and retentive memory. But if ☿ be ill dignified, the person represented will be of weak intellect, and withal a slanderer, boaster, liar, sycophant, and very much addicted to petty thieving.

☿ rules the brain, tongue, hands, and feet ; all disorders of the brain, defects of memory, imperfection of speech, headache, gout, and whatever impairs the intellectual faculties.

Employments.—He generally signifies all literary men, philosophers, mathematicians, merchants, secretaries, writers, sculptors, poets, orators, advocates, schoolmasters, stationers, printers, exchangers of money, attorneys, ambassadors, commissioners, clerks, artificers, accountants, solicitors ; sometimes thieves, prattling ministers, busybodies, grammarians, carriers, messengers, footmen, and usurers.

Luna, or the Moon

The ☽ is cold, moist, feminine, and watery, and in Horary Astrology she becomes the most powerful of all the heavenly bodies.   She produces a full stature ; fair, pale complexion ; round face, grey eyes, short arms, thick hands and feet, and a body inclined to corpulency ; and if afflicted by ☉, blemishes in or near the eye, or a peculiar weakness of sight, is often the result.

Well dignified, she makes the querent of engaging manners, easily frightened, well disposed, fond of novelties and travelling.

Her being ill dignified represents an idle, drunken, beggarly person, hating labour, and of a mean spirit.

She governs the brain, stomach, bowels, left eye of the male, and right eye of the female.

Her *Diseases* are rheumatism, consumption, complaints in the bowels, palsy, dropsy, scrofula, and lunacy, as also those diseases peculiar to young children.

Employments.—She signifies queens, countesses, ladies, and all manner of women ; as also the common people, travellers, pilgrims, sailors, fishermen, fishmongers, brewers, tapsters, publicans, coachmen, huntsmen, mariners, millers, maltsters, drunkards, oysterwives, fishwomen, charwomen, tripewomen, and generally such women as carry commodities in the streets ; as also midwives, nurses, etc., hackneymen, watermen, and waterbearers.

CHAPTER V

SIGNIFICATIONS OF THE TWELVE HOUSES

THE FIRST HOUSE.—From this house we answer all questions that concern the querent's mind, length of life, state of health, accidents, mind, and form of body ; the state of a ship at sea ; brethren of friends, fathers of kings, wives of enemies and partners, death of servants, long journeys of children, friends of brethren, and the thoughts of the querent.

THE SECOND HOUSE, all questions concerning wealth, poverty, loss, gain, money lent, moveable goods, prosperity or adversity, brethren of private enemies, fathers of friends, trade, and honour of children ; the death of wife, husband, partner, or public enemy.

THE THIRD HOUSE, all questions respecting the first brother or sister, neighbours, short journeys, letters, railways, rumours, sects, dreams, churches, clerks, children of friends and friends of children, messengers, trade of servants, sickness of kings, and private enemies of father.

THE FOURTH HOUSE.—This denotes all matters relating to fathers, houses, lands, towns, cities, hidden treasures, gardens, orchards, fields, vineyards. It denotes the *end* of every undertaking, and signifies the house of the querent ; also the wealth of the *first* brother or sister, the private enemies of children, the trade of husbands and open enemies, dead men's goods, sickness of friends and the friends of servants.

THE FIFTH HOUSE.—This house governs children,

pregnancy, the personal effects of fathers ; health and personal description of the first child ; success of messengers, pleasure, charters, lotteries, betting, horse and foot racing, dancing, music, merriment, cards, dice, the second brother or sister, death of kings, and private enemies of servants.

THE SIXTH HOUSE. — This house answers all questions relating to sickness of the querent, servants, inferiors, and low persons ; small cattle, uncles, aunts, stewards, tenants, farmers, brethren of fathers, death of friends, private enemies of wives or husbands, the first child's money, and all labourers.

THE SEVENTH HOUSE governs marriage, lawsuits, all love affairs ; description of husband or wife ; and all thefts, fugitives, and runaways ; grandfathers ; contracts, partnerships, fines ; speculations in the funds, stocks, and shares ; who is victorious in lawsuits, contests, battle ; our third brother or sister, the second child ; physicians or doctors, persons with whom you deal in business ; whether it be well to remove, public enemies, the children of brethren, the house of fathers, the substance of servants and poor people, the honour of kings, the religion of friends and their long journeys.

THE EIGHTH HOUSE, the substance of wife or husband, the querent's own death, legacies, wills, and wealth of partners, and public enemies ; brethren and neighbours of servants and their short journeys ; substance of a third brother or sister ; sickness and servants of the first brother or sister ; the private enemies of clergymen or divines ; the friends of kings, judges, and masters ; the trade or honour of friends, and the religion of private enemies.

THE NINTH HOUSE.—This rules the querent's long journeys, voyages, foreign parts, travel in foreign lands, clergymen, divines, benefices, books, printing, insurance, science, prayers, visions, omens, worship, the religion of the querent, the third child ; public enemies, lawsuits, partnerships, etc., of the *first* brother or sister ; sickness of fathers, and their servants and tenants ; fathers of servants, grand-children, the querent's first brother or sister-in-law, houses of tenants and servants ; brethren of public enemies, partners, and those with whom you deal in business ; friends of friends, private enemies of kings.

THE TENTH HOUSE relates to the querent's honour, credit, trade, profession, mother, situations or employ-ments, masters, kings, nobles, magistrates, judges, his father-in-law, the substance taken away by thieves, the fathers and houses of all persons ruled by the seventh house, the public enemies of fathers, death of the first brother or sister, first child of tenants and servants, sickness of the first child, private enemies of friends, friends of private enemies.

THE ELEVENTH HOUSE refers to the friends of the querent, his hopes, desires, advisers ; the wealth of kings, the religion of first brother or sister, the fifth brother or sister of the querent, the death of fathers, the public enemies of children, their wives, lawsuits, partners, etc. (as ruled by the seventh) ; long journeys of neighbours or first brother and sister, and step-children.

THE TWELFTH HOUSE shows sorrow, tribulation, grief, and imprisonment ; malice, persecution, suicide, treason ; large cattle ; assassination, envy, prisons ; trade and profession of first brother or sister ; sickness of wives or husbands, partners, etc. ; religion of fathers, death of children ; public enemies, etc., of servants and tenants, brethren of kings, and masters ; mother's first brother or sister, and her short journeys and the long journeys of the father.

———

NOTE.—You require to be exceedingly careful in selecting the right house for the question. Many persons sadly confuse this, and take the third house for all brethren, the fifth for all children, and so on. This is foolish ; for how can one house, and perhaps only one significator, point out the conditions of perhaps half a dozen persons ? Clearly understand at first what the querent or interrogator wants. If about his brethren, inquire if the first, second, or third, or what brother, and select your house, the same with children. Suppose a person inquired the condition of his second brother, if he had many enemies, whether he had any children, was married, etc., you would then take the fifth for the second brother (being the third house from the third house) ; the eleventh would show his public enemies, and the fourth his private enemies (being the seventh and twelfth from the fifth) ; the ninth would rule his first child (being the fifth from the fifth) ; and the eleventh for his marriage (being the seventh from the fifth). Again, if a man inquired, Is my servant pregnant ? you would take the tenth house, as it is the fifth from the sixth. Again, if he inquired, Will my servant stay with me ? then you would take the sixth house for the servant and the twelfth for her removal, for the twelfth is the seventh from the sixth. And thus you must judge in every case, otherwise you will be confused and able to judge nothing correctly.

The first, fourth, seventh, and tenth houses are called *angles*, or *angular* houses.

The second, fifth, eighth, and eleventh are termed *succeedent* houses, because they succeed the angles.

The third, sixth, ninth, and twelfth are termed *cadent* houses—that is, falling from the angles, as a planet leaving and angle enters a cadent house.

The angles are strongest, and of these the first and tenth are the most potent. The Moon in an angle, especially in a moveable sign and not " void of course," is a sure sign of a speedy termination to any matter.

A planet should not be taken as in a certain house immediately it leaves the cusp of the other house. For instance, in figure No. 2, I should consider ♅

as influencing the twelfth house and not the eleventh, because he has only just passed the cusp ; but I should take ♀ as just entering the fourth house because she is nearly 7° from the cusp of the fifth. I generally allow about 5° or 6°. A planet on a cusp is always powerful and has much signification, and should never be overlooked.

CHAPTER VI

THE NATURES, PLACES, GENERAL DESCRIPTIONS, AND DISEASES SIGNIFIED BY THE TWELVE SIGNS

Aries ♈

IT is a masculine, diurnal sign, moveable, cardinal, equinoctial sign ; in nature fiery, hot, and dry ; choleric, bestial, luxurious, intemperate, and violent ; the diurnal house of ♂ ; of the fiery triplicity, and of the east.

Diseases.—All gumboils, swellings, pimples in the face, small-pox, hare-lips, polypus, ringworms, falling sickness, apoplexies, megrims, toothache, headache, and baldness.

Places.—Where sheep and cattle feed, sandy or hilly ground ; a place of refuge for thieves (as unfrequented places) ; in houses, the covering, ceiling, or plastering ; a stable for small beasts ; lands newly taken in or recently ploughed, or where bricks or lime have been burnt.

Description or Shape of Body.—A dry body, not very tall, lean or spare, large bones, and limbs strong, the visage long, black eyebrows, a long scraggy neck, thick shoulders, the complexion dusky, brown, or swarthy.

Taurus ♉

It is an earthy, cold, dry, melancholy, feminine, nocturnal, fixed, bestial sign, of the earthy triplicity, and south ; the night house of Venus.

Diseases.—The King's evil, sore throats, wens,

fluxes of rheums falling into the throat, quinsies, abscesses in those parts.

Places.—Stables where horses are, low houses, houses where the implements of farming are laid up, pasture or feeding grounds where no houses are near, plain grounds, or where bushes have lately been eradicated and wherein corn and wheat are substituted, some little trees not far off; in houses, cellars, and low rooms.

Shape and Description.—It represents one short but stout, a strong, and well-set person; broad forehead, great eyes, large swarthy face, and broad strong shoulders, great mouth, and thick lips; gross hands, and black coarse hair.

Gemini ♊

It is an aerial, hot, moist, sanguine, diurnal, common, double-bodied, humane sign; the diurnal house of ☿ and of the airy triplicity, western and masculine.

Diseases.—It signifies all diseases, accidents, or infirmities in the arms, shoulders, or hands; corrupted blood, windiness in the veins, distempered fancies, and nervous diseases.

Places.—Wainscot of rooms, plastering, and walls and halls of houses; hills and mountains, barns, stores, houses for corn, coffers, chests, and high places.

Description.—An upright, tall, straight body, either in man or woman; the complexion sanguine, not clear but obscure and dark; long arms, yet many times the hands and feet short, and very fleshy; a dark hair, almost black; a strong active body, a good piercing hazel eye, and wanton, and of a perfect and quick sight; of excellent understanding, and judicious in worldly affairs.

Cancer ♋

It is the only house of the Moon, and is the first sign of the watery triplicity; is a watery, cold, moist, phlegmatic, feminine, nocturnal, moveable sign; mute and slow of voice; fruitful, and northern.

Diseases.—It signifies imperfections all over, or, in the breast, stomach and paps ; weak digestion, cold stomach, phthisic, salt phlegms, rotten coughs, dropsical humours, imposthumations in the stomach, cancers, which are mostly in the breasts.

Places.—The sea, great rivers, navigable rivers, but in inland countries it denotes places near rivers, brooks, springs, wells, cellars, in houses, wash houses, marsh grounds, ditches with rushes, sedges, sea banks, trenches, cisterns.

Shape and Description.—Generally a low and short stature, the upper parts larger than the lower ; a round visage ; sickly, pale, and white complexion, and the hair a sad brown ; little eyes.

Leo ♌

It is the only house of the Sun ; by nature fiery, hot, dry, choleric ; diurnal, commanding, bestial, barren, of the east, and fiery triplicity, and masculine.

Diseases.—All afflictions in the ribs and sides, as pleurisies, convulsions, pains in the back, trembling or passion of the heart, sore eyes, the plague, the pestilence, and the yellow jaundice.

Places.—A place where wild beasts frequent, woods, forests, deserts, steep, rocky, and inaccessible places, king's palaces, castles, forts, parks ; in houses where fire is kept, and near a chimney.

Shape and Form—Great round head, large prominent eyes, quick sighted ; a full and large body, and more than of middle stature ; broad shoulders, narrow sides, yellow or dark flaxen hair, curling or turned up ; a fierce countenance, but ruddy, high, sanguine complexion ; strong, valiant, and active ; step firm, and mind courteous.

Virgo ♍

It is an earthy, cold, melancholy, barren, feminine, nocturnal, southern sign ; the house and exaltation of ☿ ; and of the earthy triplicity.

Places.—It signifies a study, or where books are kept; a closet, a dairy-house, corn-fields, granaries, malt-houses, hay, barley, wheat, or pea ricks, etc.; or a place where cheese or butter is preserved and stored up.

Diseases.—The worms, wind, cholic; all obstructions and croakings of the bowels, infirmities in the testicles, and any disease in the abdomen.

Shape and Form.—A slender body, rather tall, but well composed; a ruddy, brown complexion; black hair, well favoured, but not a beautiful creature; a sharp, shrill voice, all members inclining to brevity, a witty, discreet person, judicious, and exceedingly well spoken; studious, and given to history, whether man or woman.

Libra ♎

This sign is hot and moist, sanguine, masculine, moveable, equinoctial, cardinal, humane, diurnal, of the airy triplicity, and western; the day house of ♀.

Diseases.—All diseases (or the stone and gravel) in the reins, or the back and kidneys, heat and disease in the loins and haunches; imposthumes or ulcers in the reins, kidneys, or bladder; weakness in the back, and corrupt blood.

Places.—In the fields it respresents ground near windmills, or some straggling barn, or out-house, or sawpits, or where coopers work, or wood is cut, sides of hills, tops of mountains, trees, grounds where hawking or hunting is practised; sandy and gravel fields; pure clear air; the upper rooms in houses, chambers, garrets, one chamber within another; tops of chests of drawers and wardrobes.

Shape and Form.—It personates a well framed body, straight, tall, and more subtle or slender than gross; a round, well-formed visage; sanguine colour; in youth no abundance or excess either red or white; but in age pimples, or a very high colour; the hair smooth and long, eyes generally dark, and temper even.

Scorpio ♏

It is a cold, watery, nocturnal, phlegmatic, northern feminine sign, of the watery triplicity ; the house and joy of Mars : usually it represents subtle, deceitful men.

Diseases.—Gravel, the stone in the secret parts of bladder ; ruptures, fistulas, or the piles ; priapisms, all afflictions in the private parts, either of men or women ; defects in the matrix, and its diseases ; injuries, etc., to the spermatic cord, the groin, etc.

Places.—Places where all kinds of creeping beasts use, as beetles, etc., or such as are without wings and are poisonous ; gardens, vineyards, orchards, ruinous houses near waters, muddy, moorish grounds ; stagnant lakes, quagmires, ponds, sinks, the kitchen or larder, waste house, etc.

Form and Description.—A corpulent, strong, able body, of a broad or square face, a dusky, muddy complexion, and sad, dark hair, a hairy body, somewhat bow-legged, and short-necked.

Sagittary ♐

It is of the fiery triplicity, and east ; in nature, hot, dry, masculine, choleric ; diurnal, common, bicorporal, or double body, the house and joy of ♃.

Diseases.—It rules the thighs and buttocks, and all fistulous tumours or hurts falling in those members and generally denotes heated blood, fevers pestilence, falls from horses, or hurts from them, or four-footed beasts ; also hurts from fire, heat, and intemperateness in sports.

Places.—A stable for war horses, or a house where great four-footed beasts are kept ; it represents in the fields, hills and the highest lands—also grounds that rise a little above the rest ; in houses, upper rooms and places near the fire.

Shape and Form of Body.—It represents a well-favoured countenance, somewhat long visage, but full and ruddy, or almost like sunburnt, the hair light chestnut colour, the stature somewhat above the middle size, a conformity in the members, and a strong, able body ; inclined to baldness, and one fond of horses.

Capricorn ♑

It is the house of Saturn, and is nocturnal, dry, melancholy, earthly, cold, feminine, cardinal, moveable, four-footed, southern, and the exaltation of ♂.

Diseases.—It rules the knees, and all diseases incident to those places, either by strain or fractures ; it denote leprosy, itch, and cutaneous complaints.

Places.—It shows an ox-house, or cow-house, or where calves are kept, or tools for husbandry, or old wood is laid up, or where sails for ships and such material are stored ; also sheep-pens, and grounds where sheep feed, fallow grounds, barren fields, bushy and thorny ; dung-hills in fields, or where soil is laid in low houses ; dark places, near the ground or the threshold.

Corporature.—Usually dry bodies, not high of stature, long, lean, and slender visage ; thin beard, and black hair, a narrow chin, long small neck, and narrow chest.

Aquarius ♒

This is an airy, hot, and moist sign ; diurnal, sanguine, fixed, humane, masculine, the house of ♅ and western.

Diseases.—It governs the legs, ankles, and all manner of infirmities incident to those members ; spasmodic and nervous diseases, cramp, wind, etc.

Places.—Hilly and uneven places ; spots newly dug or ploughed, or where quarries of stone are, or any minerals have been dug up ; in houses, the roofs, eaves or upper parts, vineyards, or near some little spring or conduit head.

Shape and Form.—It represents a squat, thick corporature, or one of a strong, plump, well composed body, not tall, a long visage, sanguine complexion ; if ♄, who joys in this house, be in ♑ or ♒, the party is black in hair, and in complexion sanguine, with prominent teeth ; otherwise I have observed the party is of a clear white or fair complexion, and of sandy-coloured hair, or very flaxen, and a very clear skin.

Pisces ♓

This is a northern, cold sign, fruitful, phlegmatic, feminine, watery ; the house of Jupiter, and exaltation of ♀ ; a common bicorporeal, or double-bodied sign ; an idle, effeminate, sickly sign, or representing a person of no action.

Sickness.—All diseases in the feet, as the gout ; and all lameness and pains incident to those members, mucous discharges, itch, blotches, breakings out, boils and ulcers proceeding from corrupt blood, colds and moist diseases, and bowel complaints caused by wet feet.

Places.—It represents grounds full of water, or where many springs and many fowls are ; also fish ponds, or rivers full of fish, places where hermitages have been, moats about houses and water mills ; in houses, places near the water, as some well or pump, or where some water stands.

Coporature.—A short stature, not very well made ; a large, round face, pale complexion, not very straight, but stooping somewhat with the head.

CHAPTER VII

OF THE ESSENTIAL DIGNITIES OF THE PLANETS

THE signs are distributed to the planets in the following order, and are called the planets' houses, or mansions :—

♈ and ♏ are the houses of Mars.
♉ and ♎   „   Venus.

♊ and ♍ are the houses of Mercury.
♐ and ♓   „   Jupiter.
♋ is the house of   The Moon.
♌   „   The Sun.
♑   „   Saturn.
♒   „   Uranus.

They are called " houses " or " mansions " ; for when the planets are in their respective signs, they are then much more powerful, and become lords of the figure, according to the sign that is on the ascendant. For instance, should ♈ be rising, then Mars is lord of the figure ; the same if ♏ arise. If ♐ be rising, then ♃ is lord, and so on of the others.

Moreover, there are some signs in which certain planets are found to be very powerful, though not to the same extent or degree as when in their own houses. These are called the " exaltations of the planets," and they run thus :—♈ is the exaltation of the Sun ; ♉ of the Moon ; ♋ of Jupiter ; ♍ of Mercury ; ♎ of Saturn ; ♏ of Herschel ; ♑ of Mars ; and ♓ of Venus. The signs *opposite* to these are those in which they receive their " fall," being then weak in power, and the signs *opposite* to their respective " houses " are called the " detriments " of the planets. They are then especially weak and unfortunate. For instance, ♉ and ♎ are the detriments of ♂, being in opposition to ♈ and ♏, which are the " houses " of ♂. The table on page 36 will show this at a glance.

There are other signs also, in which the planets are powerful, but only to a small extent ; and these signs agree with the planets in *nature*. For instance, ☿ joys in ♊, ♍, ♎, and ♒, being signs of a scientific nature, and most allied to his own nature : ♀ in fruitful, moist signs, as ♋ and ♓ ; ☉ and ♂ in hot, fiery signs, as ♈, ♌, or ♐. ♃ in fruitful, temperate signs, and especially in ♋ and ♓, and also in ♎ and ♒. ♄ delights in ♎ and ♒, and ♅ in ♎ and ♏. The ☽ is the same as ♀.

CHAPTER VIII

HOW TO ERECT A MAP OR FIGURE OF THE HEAVENS

FIRST look in my Ephemeris, and in the left hand page you will find a column headed " Sidereal Time." Then look what this sidereal time is for the day on which you want to erect the map or figure, and note it down. Then see if the hour for which you desire to erect the figure be *before* or *after* noon ; if *before,* you proceed thus :—Find the *difference* between this

Sign.	Planet's House.	Exalta- tion.	Tripli- city.	Fall.	Detri- ment.
♈	♂	☉ 19°	☉	♄	♀
♉	♀	☽ 3°	♀	♅	♂
♊	☿		☿		♃
♋	☽	5°	♂	♂	♄
♌	☉		☉		♅
♍	☿	☿ 15°	☽	♀	♃
♎	♀	♄ 21°	♄	☉	♂
♏	♂	♅	♂	☽	♀
♐	♃		♃		☿
♑	♄	♂ 28°	♀	♃	☽
♒	♅		♄		☉
♓	♃	♀ 27°	♂	☿	☿

hour and noon, and subtract the amount from the " sidereal time " ; if the sidereal time is not enough to make the subtraction, then add 24 hours to it, and subtract this : suppose you want a figure for half-past 8 A.M. on the 24th March, 1883, the sidereal time on that day is 0h. 6m. 28s. ; now the difference in time between 8.30 A.M. and 12 o'clock noon is 3h. 30m., therefore you subtract 3h. 30m. from the sidereal time ; but you cannot take 3h. 30m. from 0h. 6m. 28s., therefore you must add 24h. to it, and make it 24h. 6m. 28s., then subtract the 3h. 30m. from it, and you say, 0 from 28 is 28, 30 from 6 you cannot take, so you borrow 60 and say, 30 from 66, which is 36— carry one and say, 4 from 24 leaves 20, and you have left 20h. 36m. 28s. (Of course you will know there are 60 seconds in 1 minute, and 60 minutes in an hour, and this is why you borrow the 60.)

Suppose again you wanted a figure for 8h. 30m. A.M. on the 19th March, 1883. On that day the sidereal time is 23h. 46m. 46s. ; now from this you *can* take the 3h. 30m., and it will leave 20h. 16m. 46s.

But if the time for which you wish to erect a figure be *after* noon, then *add* that time to the sidereal time at noon ; if the amount exceeds 24 hours, then deduct that amount (viz., 24 hours) thus : Suppose you want a figure for 7.30 P.M. on the 24th March, 1883, the sidereal time on that day is 0h. 6m. 28s., add the 7h. 30m. to it and it amounts to 7h. 36m. 28s. But suppose it was 7.30 P.M. on the 19th March, the sidereal time on that day is 23h. 46m. 46s., add your 7h. 30m. to it, thus : 0 to 46 is 46, 30 to 46 is 76, or 1 hour 16 minutes, put down the 16 and carry the 1, then 1 and 7 are 8, and 8 and 23 are 31, and you have 31h. 16m. 46s. Now as this exceeds 24 hours, you must deduct 24 from it, and say, 24 from 31 leaves 7, and you will have left 7h. 16m. 46s.

Now this amount is what we call the sidereal time, or right ascension of the meridian (they both mean the same thing), at 7.30 P.M. on the 19th March, 1883, and the 7h. 36m. 28s. is the same for the 24th March at 7.30 P.M.

Now, when you have done as stated, and got the sidereal time for the time you want your figure, refer to the " Tables of Houses " at the end of the Ephemeris, and use that table which is nearest to the latitude of the place in which you live. If you live at Manchester or in Yorkshire, etc., use the Liverpool tables, but if near London, then use the London tables. Suppose you live in London, then look in the table of houses, and in the column marked " Sidereal Time " for 7h. 36m. 28s., or the nearest amount thereto ; the nearest to this you will find in the bottom division of the first page, and it is 7h. 35m. 5s   Now, in the next column to that on the right is 22, and at the top of that column you will find 10 and the sign of ♋, the 10 means the 10th house, or midheaven, and ♋ means that that sign and the 22nd degree of it are then transiting the meridian ; you therefore place ♋ 22° on the cusp of the 10th house.   In the next small column you find 27, and at the top 11 and ♌, which means that it is the 11th house, and that ♌ 27° is then on the cusp of it.   In the next column you will find 26, and at the top 12 and ♍, the 12 means the 12th house, and ♍ 26° are the sign and degree on its cusp, and you place them there accordingly.   In the next column, which is wider than the others, you find 16° 45', and at the top ascen. ♎ ; the ascen. means the ascendant, or 1st house, or the Eastern horizon, and the table denotes that 16° 45' of the sign ♎ were rising at the hour and minute aforesaid, viz., 7h. 30m. P.M. on the 24th March, 1883.   In the next small column you find 13, and at the top 2 ♎, the 2 means the 2nd house ; but if you look slowly down that column you will find that ♎ runs out, and ♏ begins, you therefore place ♏ 13° on the cusp of the 2nd house.   In the next column you find 15, and at the top 3 and ♏, the 3 means the 3rd house ; look down this column, as you did the other, and you see ♏ runs out and ♐ begins, and you therefore put ♐ 15° on the cusp of the 3rd house.   You have now got the signs and degrees on six, or half of the houses, and on the other six you put the *same* degrees, but *opposite* signs.   The signs are thus :—

♈ Aries is opposite ♎ Libra.
♉ Taurus   ,,   ♏ Scorpio.

♊ Gemini is opposite ♐ Sagittarius.
♋ Cancer   ,,   ♑ Capricorn.
♌ Leo   ,,   ♒ Aquarius.
♍ Virgo   ,,   ♓ Pisces.

Therefore on the cusp of the 4th house you put ♑ 22°, for ♑ is opposite ♋ ; on the 5th house you put ♒ 27°, as ♒ is opposite ♌ ; on the 6th you put ♓ 26°, for ♓ is opposite ♍ ; on the 7th you put ♈ 16° 45', for ♈ is opposite ♎ ; on the 8th you put ♉ 13°, for ♉ is opposite ♏ ; and on the 9th you put ♊ 15°, for this sign is opposite to ♐. Now, you have the signs and degrees on all the houses. (See the *second* figure.)

NOTE.—Owing to the latitude of our country being a great way North, the signs rise irregularly, that is some rise quicker than others, and their rising thus often results in *one* sign occupying the cusps of *two* houses, in this case there are always *two* signs " *intercepted*," that is, between the cusps of two houses. Suppose, for instance, our sidereal time was 18h. 34m. 51s. (look in the fourth segment of the " Tables for London "), we find ♑ 8° on the 10th, ♑ 27° on the 11th, ♒ 25° on the 12th, ♈ 20-34 on the ascendant, ♉ 29° on the 2nd, ♊ 20° on the 3rd ; therefore you see ♑ occupies the cusps of the 10th and 11th houses, and if you read the signs over in rotation—thus : ♈ ♉ ♊ ♋, etc.—you will find no ♍, but ♌ on the 6th and ♎ on the 7th, and as ♍ follows ♌, it must be placed in the *middle* of the 6th house ; you put the sign here, but *no degrees*, as it does not occupy a cusp, and as ♓ is opposite to ♍, and the 12th house is opposite the 6th ; you must place the sign ♓ in the middle of the 12th house. See Figure 1 on the following page, which will explain how these signs are placed.

It will sometimes happen that even four signs are intercepted, and which is generally when ♐, ♑, or ♒ is rising ; they must then be placed precisely as shown, and in the middle of the house in which they fall, according to the order of the signs.

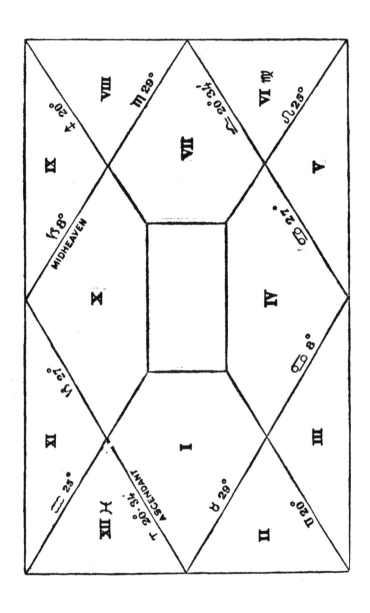

In calculating the aspects of the planets, intercepted signs must always be reckoned the same as the other signs, viz., 30° for each sign.

The fact that a sign is intercepted does not interfere with its potency in describing a person or event.

At and near the Equator, all the signs rise in regular rotation ; thus, if ♈ 15° were on the 10th house ♉ 15° would be on the 11th, ♊ 15° on the 12th, and the other signs on the other houses in like manner.

CHAPTER IX

HOW TO PLACE THE PLANETS IN THE FIGURE

In my Ephemeris the longitudes of all the planets are given for noon on each day.   First observe if the time of the figure is for A.M. or P.M. ; if for A.M., find the motion of the planet from the noon *previous* ; but if P.M., then take the noon *after* : whatever this motion is, you proceed with it as follows, and say—

As 24h. is to the *time from noon* of the figure, so is the planet's motion.   Multiply the 2nd and 3rd terms together, and divide by the first, and the quotient will be the amount of the planet's motion for the time of the figure, which you must subtract from the long. at noon if the time be A.M., and *add* if it be P.M., unless the planet be retrograde (which you will see by a great ℞ in the Ephermeris) when you *add* for A.M. time, and *subtract* for P.M. time.

On the 24th March, 1883, we find the Sun's longitude to be 3° ♈ 31' 1" ; and as our time is 7.30 P.M., we take the noon of the 25th (had it been *before* noon of the 24th we should have taken the noon of the 23rd) and his long. then is 4° ♈ 30' 24".   Subtract the 3° ♈ 31' 1" from this, and there remains 0° 59' 23", which is the motion of the Sun for 24 hours, or one day.   We therefore say, as 24 hours is to 7h. 30m., so is 59' 23".   Multiply the second and third terms together, and divide by the first, and you get the

answer, which is 18' 33". Add this to his long. at
noon, which will make it 3° 49' 34", and you have his
exact long. at 7.30 P.M., on the 24th March, 1883.
With the Moon you can do the same, or take her long.
at midnight on the 24th, instead of noon on the 25th,
thus—

☽'s long. at noon on 24th   -   11° ♎ 37'
    „   midnight, 24th   -   17° ♎ 31'

Difference   -   -   5°   54'

which is her motion in 12 hours, then say—As 12 hours
is to 7h. 30m., so is 5° 54', and you get the answer,
3° 39', which you add to her long. at noon (11° ♎ 37'),
and you get 15° ♎ 16', which is her correct long. at
7.30 P.M. on the 24th.

Proceed with the planets exactly as shown for the
Sun ; with ♆, ♅, and ♄ it is hardly necessary,
because their motions are so little that they can be
proportioned in the head, thus—the long. of ♄ on
24th is 22° ♉ 41', on the 25th, 22° ♉ 47'—difference,
6'. Now, 7h. 30m. is nearly a third of 24 hours ; and
if you take a third of 6', it will be 2'. Add the 2' to
the 22° ♉ 41', and you have 22° ♉ 43', ♄'s true
place at 7.30 P.M.

If you wish for expedition and dispatch, use
Logarithms and proceed thus. Take ☿, for instance:

Long. at noon on 24th   -   -   13° ♓ 21'
                    25th   -   -   14°   58'

Difference -   -   •   1°   37'
Proportional Log. of 1° 37'   -   1·17159
    „   „   of 7h. 30m.   -   0·50515

Log. of ☿'s motion   -   0°   30'   1·67674
Add thereto   -   -   13° ♓ 21'

and you have   13° ♓ 51',   which is the
true long. of ☿ at 7.30 P.M.

The Rule is, add the proportional Logarithm of the planet's daily motion to the proportional Logarithm of the time required, and the sum will be the Logarithm of the motion required. *Add* this to the planet's place at noon, if the time be P.M. ; but *subtract* if A.M., and the sum will be the planet's true

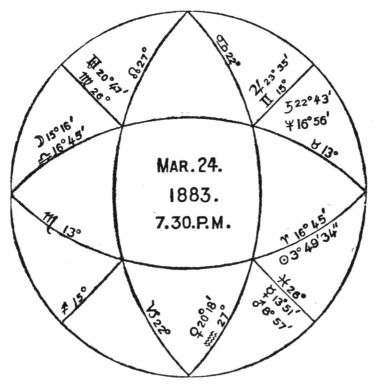

place. Should the planet be *Retrograde*, subtract for P.M., and add for A.M.

The Sun's longitude we found to be 3° ♈ 49' 34", so we place him in the middle of the 6th house. The Moon's long. is 15° ♎ 16', and she will be just above the ascendant, for 15° 16' of a sign will rise before 16° 45' ; hence the Moon has just risen, or is just above the horizon. The long. of ♅ will be 16° ♉ 56' ; hence he should be put just inside the 8th house ; and ♄ is

22° 43′ of the same sign, so we put him at the top of ♅, and the other planets are placed as seen in the figure on page 43.   You can make your figures any shape or form you like, so long as there are twelve divisions.

CHAPTER X

HOW MATTERS ARE BROUGHT TO PERFECTION

FIRST by ☌, when the lord of the ascendant and the lord of the house ruling the matter or person are hastening to a ☌ and in angles and moveable signs, and forming the ☌ before either meets with an aspect from another planet ; if the planets are swift in motion, so much the quicker will it come to pass ; if the ☌ occurs in succeedent houses, then the matter will be much slower in coming to perfection, and if in the cadent houses, slower still ; yet, if the lords meet by ☌ without frustration or impediment, the matter *will be* brought to perfection, but by a very slow process, and will drag along heavily, and there will be great loss of time and shuffling.

Next, by the ⚹ or △. If the principal significators are applying by a ⚹ or △, angular, and strong essentially and no malevolent planet intervenes, then the matter inquired about will be brought to perfection. If the significators apply by ☐ there will be difficulty, a lot of suspicion one of the other, hankering and doubt, but if the planets be angular and strong, the matter will be brought to perfection with or without difficulty ; but if the significators apply by a ☐, and in succeedent or cadent houses, the parties will quarrel, and the thing will not be brought to a satisfactory conclusion.

If the significators are in ☍ they denote envy, enmity, and that the querent or quesited shall be detrimented by the person or matter inquired about, and whichever significator is the weaker of the two, that person will suffer the damage.

Translation.—Things are brought to perfection by translation of light. Suppose the significators are separating from an aspect, and another planet aspects favourably one significator, and immediately applies to and aspects the other ; such is called *translation of light.* This third planet shows that the matter will be brought to perfection by a third party, and the house occupied or ruled by this third planet shows the person that shall bring it about, as, if the 3rd house, a neighbour, the 4th, a father, 5th, children, and so on of the others. The ☽ is the most powerful translator of light.

Collection.—Matters are also brought to perfection by " Collection," that is, when both the principal significators do not behold or aspect each other, but both cast their rays to a more *weighty planet* than themselves, and they both receive this planet in some of their dignities, then that planet which thus *collects* both their lights brings the thing to perfection, and the person signified by this planet shall be the one who brings it to perfection, as many times you see two at variance or cannot make a bargain, when suddenly a friend or neighbour comes in and reconciles all differences.

CHAPTER XI

HOW MATTERS ARE FRUSTRATED, IMPEDITED, OR NOT BROUGHT TO PERFECTION

WHEN the two significators (viz., that of the querent, and that of the quesited or matter enquired about), are applying by ☌ or other good aspect, and before the aspect is completed another planet aspects one of the significators, then the thing is hindered or frustrated, and the position of this 3rd planet shows through what or whom the matter will be frustrated. as, if it be lord of the 2nd, it will be money, lord of the 3rd, neighbours or brethren or journeys, lord of the 4th, the father, etc. But if this planet applies to the significator of the matter, or quesited, then you judge it differently, reckoning the house ruling the matter as the *first*; for instance, if it be about a partner (ruled by the 7th), and the frustrating planet be lord of the 8th, then it will be the partner's money that stops him ; if the 10th, then his father, etc., and so on of the other houses.

Refranation.—This is when the two significators are applying to ♂ or good aspect of each other, and before the aspect is completed one of the two turns *retrograde*, so the aspect is not completed—that significator who turns ℞ denotes the party who will back out, or shirk the matter.

Impediment is when the significators are evilly placed by being cadent in their debilities, or aspected by the malefics. They then signify innumerable difficulties, so that the matter in hand cannot be carried through.

Study these two chapters well, for upon them depends the vital part of the answer.

CHAPTER XII

OF THE MEASURE OF TIME

MOVEABLE	signs on	angles	denote	days.
,,	,,	succeedents	,,	weeks.
,,	,,	cadents	,,	months.
Common	,,	angles	,,	weeks.
,,	,,	succeedents	,,	months
,,	,,	cadents	,,	years.
Fixed	,,	angles	,,	months.
,,	,,	succeedents	,,	years.
,,	,,	cadents	,,	unknown.

Example.—Suppose the ☽ in ♎ 16° in an angle, and applying to ☿ in ♐ 20°, the difference between the two is 4° ; hence the event signified by ☽ ∗ ☿ would occur in 4 days ; but if the ☽ had been in ♏ 16° in an angle, and applying to ☿, it would have been 4 months

ere the event occurred, for fixed signs on angles denote
months. Always take the planet which *applies*, and
not the one applied to, for the measure of time. This
is a difficult thing to judge exact, unless the planets
be on the cusps of houses ; for instance, the ☽ in ♈
on the cusp of the 10th, denotes days ; but if ☽ were
in ♈ in the middle of the 10th, it would be longer
time, for the time gradually increases from a day on
the cusp to a week on the cusp of the 11th, and from
a week on the cusp of the 11th, to a month on the
cusp of the 12th, that is for moveable signs ; and the
other signs and houses are to be dealt with in a similar
manner, according to the locality of the planet.

CHAPTER XIII

THE DIRECTION OF THE HOUSES

THE 1st East.	The 5th N.N.W.	The 9th S.W.W.
,, 2nd E.N.E.	,, 6th W.N.W.	,, 10th South.
,, 3rd N.N.E.	,, 7th West.	,, 11th S.S.E.
,, 4th North.	,, 8th W.S.W.	,, 12th E.S.E.
♈ East.	♌ E. by N.	♐ E. by S.
♉ S. by E.	♍ S. by W.	♑ South.
♊ W. by S.	♎ West.	♒ W. by N.
♋ North.	♏ N. by E.	♓ N. by W.

These mean that the direction in which one should
look for anything, is shown thus—Suppose you want
to know in what direction a certain party or thing is,
then observe the position of the lord of that party or
thing, and his position will show you in what direction
it is ; if ☿ signified the thing or person enquired about,
and occupied the first house in ♈, then it would
indicate due East ; but if in ♋ and the 7th house,
the N.W., because ♋ is North, and the 7th West,
and by mixing the two they show N.W.—the same
of all the others. These are more to be applied in
cases of theft, cattle strayed, lost children, and such
things as are lost or gone astray.

CHAPTER XIV

CONSIDERATIONS

WHEN the last 3°, or the first 3°, of a sign are rising, it is not safe to judge ; also, when the Moon is void of course ; that is, when she forms no aspect with any planet before she leaves the sign, and especially if she is just about leaving it. I have often found that in a case like this, the querent relinquishes his object, alters his mind, etc., so that nothing comes of the matter ; also, if you find evil planets on the cusp of the 6th, your answer shall give but poor satisfaction to the querent. Again, if the Moon be cadent, and especially in the 6th house, the matter in hand drags on heavily, and comes to nought in the end ; and more especially will this be the case if the ☽ be in ♏ or ♑.

Respecting the proper time to set a figure

For all matters relating to yourself, the figure should be set for the moment the *first thought* strikes you, or the moment you *first* hear, see, or think of anything, then the ascendant will represent you ; the 2nd, your money ; the 3rd, your neighbours, and brethren, journeys, etc., and so on of the other houses ; but if a person comes to you, you must not take the time you first see him, but the time when he first broaches the subject, and if a letter, the time when you first read the important part ; in short, the moment you have the *first* intimation, or cognisance of anything, is the correct time.

Note this.—In matters of buying and selling, the 1st shows the seller, and the 7th the buyer ; so if you are asked to buy anything, the 1st is for the *seller*, and the 7th the *buyer* ; and if the offer is by letter, the same will hold good.

This is a very important subject, and unless well understood, will result in grave errors and confusion. Never set a figure for the *commencement* of anything ;

but always set it for the moment the *first impression* strikes the mind, then in nine cases out of ten you will find an aspect between your lord and the lord of the house ruling the matter, and which will admit of an easy definition or judgment. Again, never set two or more figures for one matter ; the first is the only reliable one, be it bad or good.

If you are applied to by another, either personally or by letter, and do not find your figure clear, then do not judge, for the querent has not a clear idea of what he wants ; his thoughts are confused, and he is wondering what question he shall ask, or he asks for curiosity. It is seldom, indeed, that I have had a confused figure with a clear, straightforward question.

If you attend strictly to the foregoing, half the troubles and difficulties in this branch of the science will vanish.

CHAPTER XV

OF MARKS, SCARS, AND MOLES

THE sign ascending gives a mark, scar, or mole on the part of body ruled by that sign ; the sign in which the lord of the 1st is will give another ; the sign on the cusp of the 6th will give another ; the sign occupied by the lord of the 6th another ; and the sign in which the Moon is denotes another ; Herschel, Saturn, or Mars in aspect to these lords or the Moon will give another, on the part ruled by the signs they are in. If the sign or planet be masculine, it will be on the right side, if feminine, on the left ; if the signs or planets be above the earth, then the blemish is on the front part of the body, but if under the earth, behind. If the planets be in the early degrees of a sign, or the first degrees of a sign occupy the cusps aforesaid, then the mark will be on the upper part of the member ; if the planets be in the middle of signs, or the middle of signs occupy the cusps aforesaid,

5

then the blemish will be on the middle part of the member; but if the latter part of the signs be occupied as aforesaid, then the blemishes will be on the lower part of the member.

These remarks refer to such persons as are signified by the 1st house. If a brother be enquired about, judge the 3rd as the 1st, and the other houses accordingly; if a servant or tenant, take the 6th as the 1st, and the 11th as the 6th (being the sixth from the 6th), and judge accordingly; if a wife, partner, or any other person ruled by the 7th, take the 7th as the 1st, and the 12th as the 6th, and judge of the lords and signs accordingly.

Example.—In Figure No. 2 we find ♎ rising, which denotes a mole on the reins or loins, and as the middle of ♎ is rising, it would be on the middle part: the lord of the 1st (♀) is in ♒, shows a mark or mole on the ankle, or leg; the sign on the 6th is ♓, and the latter degrees denote a mark on the foot near the toes; the lord of the 6th in ♊ denotes a mark on the middle part of the arm.

If the enquiry were about a brother-in-law, he would be signified by the 9th (being the third from the 7th), and ♊ there would give a mark or mole on the middle part of the arm; and ♏ on the 6th would give another on the genitals, the lord of the 1st in ♓ would give another on the bottom of the foot near the middle part. The colour of the moles or spots can be ascertained by referring to the colours ruled by the planets and signs.

Signs and Houses ruling the Body

1st house or	♈	—Head and face.
2nd	♉	—Neck and throat.
3rd	♊	—Arms, hands, and shoulders.
4th	♋	—Breasts and stomach.
5th	♌	—Sides and back.
6th	♍	—Bowels and belly.
7th	♎	—Reins and loins.

8th house or ♏—Secret members.
9th   ,,   ♐—Hips and thighs.
10th   ,,   ♑—Knees and loins.
11th   ,,   ♒—Legs and ankles.
12th   ,,   ♓—Feet and toes.
The Masculine signs are—♈ ♊ ♌ ♎ ♐ ♒
,, Feminine   ,,   ♉ ♋ ♍ ♏ ♑ ♓

CHAPTER XVI

COLOURS SIGNIFIED BY THE PLANETS

♅—Checks and mixed colours.
♄—Black.
♃—Green, spotted, or ash coloured.
♂—Red, scarlet.
☉—Saffron, or yellow, sandy.
♀—White or bluish.
☿—Grey or dove coloured.
☽—White, cream, or pale green.
♅ and ♄—Dark plaids.
♅ and ♃—Green plaids.
♅ and ♂—Scarlet plaids.
♅ and ☉—Yellow or spotted plaids.
♅ and ♀—Blue plaids.
♅ and ☿—Light blue, or mixed plaids.
♅ and ☽—Very light plaids.
♄ and ♃—Dark green.
♄ and ♂—Dark brown.
♄ and ☉—Dark yellow, bronze colour.
♄ and ♀—Whitish grey.
♄ and ☿—Dark grey, or blue.
♄ and ☽—Deep grey, or russet.
♃ and ♂—Tawny, with light spots.
♃ and ☉—Very deep shining red.
♃ and ♀—Greenish grey.
♃ and ☿—Spotted green.
♃ and ☽—Bright, fine green.
♂ and ☉—Deep shining red,

♂ and ♀—Light red, or crimson.
♂ and ☿—Red tawny.
♂ and ☽—Light red.
☉ and ♀—Olive colour.
☉ and ☿—Light grey.
☉ and ☽—Light yellow, or green.
♀ and ☿—Purple, or light mixture.
♀ and ☽—Light blue, or bluish white.
☿ and ☽—Buff, or fawn colour.

The meaning of this is, that when a planet is in the house of another planet, you are to judge of him as mixed with that planet—thus : ♅ in ♌, the house of the ☉, would signify the dress of the quesited, or person enquired about, to be yellow or spotted plaid, or large yellow checks.

Colours of the Signs

♈—White, mixed with red.
♉ —White, mixed with lemon.
♊—White, mixed with red.
♋—Green, or russet.
♌—Red or green.
♍—Black, speckled with blue.
♎—Black, or dark crimson.
♏—Brown.
♐ —Yellow.
♑—Black or russet, dull brown.
♒—Sky blue.
♓—White.

If a planet be in its own sign, and not in aspect to another, then the quesited will be dressed in all one colour, thus : ♄ in ♑ would denote a person all in black, ♂ in ♈ a person in red or scarlet, with stripes of white.

♀ in ♒ a light sky blue ; but if ♀ had an aspect of ♂ then some red or scarlet would appear in the dress ; if with ♄, some black, and so on of all the others.

CHAPTER XVII

PROBABLE NAMES SIGNIFIED BY THE PLANETS

WHATEVER planet be taken as significators, see if it be in any kind of aspect with another planet ; if it be not, that planet whose house it is in, is the planet that forms the name.

Significator.	Aspect or House.		Name.
♄	with	☉	George, Elizabeth, or Julia.
♄		♀	William.
♄		☽ & ♀	Joan.
♃		♄	Thomas.
♃	alone		Rachel.
♃	with	☉	John or Richard.
♂		☉	Robert or Peter.
♂	alone		Anthony.
♂	with	☿	Catherine.
☉	alone		Roger, Philip, James, Stephen, Ann.
☉	with	♃	Lawrence or Lucy.
☉		♄	Andrew.
☉		♀	Alice, Maud, or Matilda.
☉		☿	Benjamin, Margaret, or Edith.
♀		♄	Isabella.
♀		☿	Agnes.
☿		♂	Matthew.
☿		♂ & ☉	Christiana.
☿		☉	Clement.
☽		♄	Nicholas.
☽		♂ & ☉	Mary.
☽		♀	Ellen.
☽	alone		Eleanor.
☽	with	☿	Simon.

♃, the ☉, and ♂ denote short names ; if they be
angular and near the midheaven, the name begins
with A or E. ♄ or ♀ gives long names.

CHAPTER XVIII

COUNTRIES RULED BY THE TWELVE SIGNS OF THE ZODIAC.

Aries.—Britain, Germany, Lower Poland, Bur-
gundy, Denmark, Palestine, Syria, and Judea,
Cities—Naples, Capua, Verona, Florence, Marseilles,
Cracow, and Leicester.

Taurus.—Persia, Media, Georgia, Asia Minor,
Archipelago, Cyprus, Poland, Ireland, and White
Russia. Cities—Dublin, Mantua, Leipsic, Parma,
and Palermo.

Gemini.—Tripoli, Armenia, Lower Egypt, Flanders,
Lombardy, Sardinia, Belgium, the West of England,
and the United States of America. Cities—London,
Versailles, Mentz, Cordova, and Nuremburg.

Cancer.—North and Western Africa, Scotland,
Holland, New Zealand, and Anatolia. Cities—
Amsterdam, Cadiz, Constantinople, Venice, York,
New York, Milan, and Manchester.

Leo.—Italy, Sicily, France, the Alps, Bohemia,
Chaldea, Sidon, and Tyre. Cities—Bath, Bristol,
Taunton, Damascus, Bolton, Portsmouth, and Phila-
delphia.

Virgo.—Turkey, Croatia, Mesopotamia, Assyria,
Greece, Thessaly, Livadia, Corinth, Morea, Switzer-
land. Cities—Jerusalem, Paris, Basle, Lyons, Reading, Bagdad, and Cheltenham.

Libra.—China, Japan, the Caspian, Thibet, Livonia,
Austria, Savoy, and Upper Egypt. Cities—Antwerp,
Lisbon, Frankfort, Vienna, and Charleston.

Scorpio.—Algiers, Bavaria, Barbary, Judea, Fez,
Morocco, and Norway. Cities—Ghent, Liverpool,
and Messina.

Sagittary.—Arabia, Dalmatia, Hungary, Spain, Slavonia, Moravia. Cities—Buda, Naples, Sheffield, Narbonne, Rotenberg, Stutland, and Cologne.

Capricorn.—India, Circan, Macian, Punjaub, Thrace, Bosnia, Bulgaria, Albania, Saxony, Hesse, Mexico, and Lithuania. Cities—Oxford, Bradenburg, and Fayence.

Aquarius.—Stony Arabia, Prussia, Red Russia, Tartary, Circassia, Wallachia, Sweden, and Abyssinia. Cities—Hamburg, Bremen, Trent, and Saltsburg.

Pisces.—Portugal, Calabria, Normandy, Gallicia (in Spain), and Nubia. Cities—Alexandria, Worms, Seville, Silicia, and Tiverton.

PART II

CHAPTER I

1. *Is the person inquired about at home ?*—See what
house signifies or rules this person, and the lord of
this house angular, the person is at home ; if the ruler
be in succeedent houses he is a little way off but can
be found, but if cadent he is away and will not be
found. If the significators of the querent and
quesited be applying to a favourable aspect, and
without frustration or impediment, then the parties
will meet ; or if there be translation of light the
querent will hear of the quesited, and from the person
signified by the translator.

2. *Shall I live long ?*—If you find the Sun, Moon,
and Ascendant free from affliction, and the two
former in any house but the 4th, 6th, or 8th, you may
judge you will ; the more so if ♃ or ♀ be in favourable
aspect to the Moon, and the malefics be in obscure
houses (viz., the 6th, 8th, and 12th), and not in any
aspect to the lights. The querent will not live long
if the lord of the 1st be in the 4th or 8th, or the ☉
and ☽ afflicted by the malefics from the 6th or 8th
houses, or the malefics holding the chief angles (1st,
7th, and 10th), and the lord of the ascendant, and
lights in obscure houses.

3. *How long am I likely to live ?*—Have regard to
the lord of the ascendant, if it apply to a ☌ , □, or ☍
of ☉, or a malefic in the 4th or 8th, then the number
of degrees between the significator and the aspect will
show the length of time he will live, according to the
measure of time explained in Part I. The ☉ or ☽ in
the 8th, going to ☌, □, or ☍ of ♄ or ♂, is a sure
sign of short life.

4. *Of an event suddenly happening whether good or evil ?*—Consider the lord of the ascendant, the ☉ and the ☽, and which planets dispose of them, and if you find them in good aspect to each other, or to ♃ or ♀, then no harm will come to the querent, but if you find ♄, ♂, or ♅ afflicting the lord of the ascendant, ☉ or ☽, then it will damage the native, and if you consider the afflicting planet and its lord you will see through whom or what the damage will come, as the 3rd house, brethren, neighbours, etc. ; 4th, fathers, lands, etc., and so on of the others.

5. *Whether an absent one be dead or alive ?*—If the absent person be a relative, then take the house signifying that relative, as the 3rd for a brother, 4th, a father, 5th, a child, etc., and if a friend take the 11th, but if no relation, nor yet a friend, take the 7th ; if you find the lord of the house ruling the quesited in the 8th or 4th, and afflicted by the malefics by ♂, □, or ☍, then the person is dead or dying ; if the aspect is just past he is just dead ; if applying he will die when the aspect is completed. If the lord of the house ruling the quesited be in the 6th, then he is ill, and the more or less his significator is afflicted, the more severe, or light, is his sickness ; and if the lord of the 4th or 8th be applying by an ill aspect to the significator in the 6th, it denotes death, but if the aspects are separating, he is getting better and will recover ; if none of these testimonies are found, then judge the quesited is alive, and well in health, more especially if his ruler be well placed and in good aspect of ☽, ☉, or ♃. If you find him alive, and wish to know when you will hear from him, then see when the lord of your 11th comes to the ✶ or △ of his significator, and about that time you will hear from, or about, him.

6. *Of a ship at sea.*—The ascendant and ☽ denote the ship, the lord of the ascendant her crew, and the lord of the 10th the captain ; if the lord of the 8th be an evil planet, and in the ascendant, or the lord of

the ascendant in the 8th, or afflicted by the lords of
the 8th, 12th, 4th, or 6th, or if the ☽ be combust, you
may judge the ship is lost, and the crew drowned ;
but if you find *reception* between the significators
aforesaid, then the ship is lost, but some of the crew
saved ; but if the ascendant, its lord, and ☽ be free
from affliction, then the ship and cargo are both safe.
Figures set for the time of sailing are not reliable in
the present state of our knowledge of astrology, for
many sail at the same instant, and some may escape
and others be wrecked.   We do not know sufficient
of the " Zodiac," and the quality of each degree, to
judge accurately from the time of sailing.

7. *Will the voyage be prosperous ?*—The ascendant
and its lord, also the ☽ fortunate, and in good aspect
to the ☉ or ♃, then the voyage will be fortunate ;
but if none of these occur, and no affliction, then the
voyage will not be a *very* fortunate one ; but should
the malefics afflict the ascendant, its lord, or the
Moon, a disastrous voyage is to be feared.   If the
afflicting planet be ruler of the 12th, there will be
danger of pirates, and if the lords of 10th and 1st be
in ☍, the crew will mutiny, and whichever ruler is the
strongest of the two, that party will overcome.

8. *Will the voyage be long or short ?*—The lord of the
9th, angular, and in a moveable sign, argues a short
voyage ; but if cadent, or just entering a fixed sign,
or slow in motion, then will the voyage be long and
tedious ; or if the ☽ be fixed and cadent, it will be
long ; but if she be angular and swift it will be short.
If the lord of the 9th be ℞ or ☽ applies to a ℞ planet,
then the vessel will return before it reaches its
destination, and if the malefics are afflicting, it will
be damaged, and meet cross winds.

9. *Will my health be better ?*—If the lord of the
ascendant and the ☽ be *leaving* the malefics, and not
in the 4th, 6th, or 8th, it will improve ; but if in the
6th and afflicted, or applying to any evil aspect, it
will not become better, but the reverse, and if the

lord of the 1st be in the 8th or 4th, and weak, death
is to be feared.

10. *Which way must I steer for better health ?*—See
where the lord of the ascendant is, and what planets
are in favourable aspect, and if these planets be not
in an evil house, and strong, to that quarter let him
steer ; if the planets be malefics he will benefit a little,
but not much, but if the ⊙ or ♃, then will his health
greatly improve ; the direction will be shown by the
house and sign the planet occupies that makes the
favourable aspect, as, if in the 10th in ♑ he should
go due S. You may be puzzled to know how to
proceed if ♎ be the sign occupied and also *rising*,
which would signify due east and west, for the first
house is east and ♎ west. I may say that if any one
ask the question seriously and earnestly, and take a
figure for the proper time, this disposition of the
planets will never occur.

11. *What part of life is likely to be most fortunate ?*—
See the positions of the Sun, Moon, Jupiter, and ♀
for if these be in the 10th, 11th, 12th, or 1st, then the
early part up to 30 years will be the best, if you find
them in the 9th, 8th, or 7th, then from 30 to 40, in the
2nd or 3rd from 40 to 50, and in the 4th, 5th, or 6th
at the end of life. If you find the ⊙, ☽, ♃, or ♀
scattered, or in different parts of the figure, then the
native's fortune, either good or bad, will be pretty
even all through life.

12. *What part of the world shall I do best in ?*—See
which planet is the strongest, whether ♃, ♀, ⊙, or ☽,
and what sign it occupies, and the direction it is in,
and what countries are ruled by that sign in the
direction indicated, and in such a part will the querent
do best. If you find two or more of these planets
angular and strong, so much the better, but always
take the *strongest* planet to signify the country, and
the direction it is in.

13. *Which way shall I meet with better success ?*—
Have regard to the lords of the ascendant and second

house, and the Moon, and see what good aspects **they** form to the fortunes, for the places of these (♃, ♀, or ☉) will signify the best direction to go. If you want a situation take the lord of 10th instead of the 2nd ; but if these lords or the ☽ are about to meet evil aspects or planets, do not move, but remain where you are. The best sign is, when the lords of 1st and 2nd, or the ☽ are separating from the malefics and applying to the benefics ; the location of the latter will then show the exact spot to which you ought to do.

CHAPTER II

OF QUESTIONS RELATING TO THE SECOND HOUSE

1. *Shall I become rich ?*—The lords of the ascendant and 2nd house strong, by essential dignity, and in elevation, in favourable aspect to the ☉, ♃, or ☽, and these planets not afflicted, the querent will become rich ; the ☽ or ♃ well aspected in the 2nd house or M.C. ; the ☉, ☽, and ♃ in trine to each other ; also if the lord of the ascendant be in the 2nd, strong and well aspected ; but if you do not find any of these testimonies then the querent will not become rich, and should ♄ hold the 2nd house, and be ℞ and but of essential dignity he will be poor, the same if the lord of the ascendant or 2nd, ♃ or the ☽, be afflicted or afflict each other. All the planets in the 5th and 6th houses are unfavourable. ♃ or the ☽ strong in the 4th is beneficial, and denotes that in the latter part of his life he will become rich.

2. *By whom or what shall I mostly gain or lose ?*— Observe where the favourable and unfavourable planets are placed with respect to house, and of what houses they are lords, and the matters and persons ruled by these houses, will show by whom or what the querent will benefit or lose. For instance, if ♃ be in the 7th, or ruler of this house, he will gain by trade,

business, partnership, law, etc., but if ♄ be there he will lose by these very means. The lord of the 1st in the 2nd, he will benefit by his own labour and industry ; if in the 3rd, and well aspected by its lord, then he will gain by brethren, short journeys, and things ruled by the 3rd ; if in the 5th, and well aspected by its lord, by racing, betting, games, etc. ; and so on of the other houses ; but if any of these lords afflict the lord of the 1st or 2nd, or both, he will lose. For instance, the lord of the 6th afflicting the lord of the 2nd, denotes loss through tenants, small cattle, servants, labourers, sickness, or matters ruled by this house ; if it be the lord of the 9th, it would signify loss through brothers-in-law, long journeys, or other matters ruled by that house.

3. *Shall I obtain the money lent ?*—The 1st and 2nd houses are for the querent, and the 7th and 8th for the person to whom the money was lent, unless it be a relative, when select the house signifying that relative, and the next to it for his money ; as if a brother, take the 3rd for him and the 4th for his money. If you find the lords of these houses in angles, and not afflicted, the money will be paid ; the same if the lords of the 2nd and 8th are going to a favourable aspect, or if the lord of the 2nd be in ☌, ✶, or △ of ♃, and there be no malefic in the 2nd or 8th house ; but if you find the lord of the 8th afflicted it is a doubtful sign, denoting that the borrower is in trouble, and if this lord be weak accidentally, or essentially, the money will not be paid ; or if the lords of the 2nd and 8th are in bad aspect, or in no aspect at all, or the infortunes in these houses, and afflicting the Moon, the money will not be paid.

The same rules apply to questions respecting payment for goods sold, or debts owing.

4. *Shall I be able to borrow the money ?*—If from a relative take the house signifying this relative, and the next one for his money ; otherwise take the 7th and 8th, and the 1st and 2nd for yourself ; then if

you find these lords in good aspect, or the lord of your
1st or 2nd in his 2nd, and the planets ruling the
quesited strong and not afflicted, you will get the
money. If the Moon, be in favourable aspect with
the lords of the 2nd and 8th, and the latter planet
strong, you will get it, but if the lord of the 8th be
weak, ℞, or afflicted, then the quesited has not the
money to lend ; if the lord of the 8th be strong but
combust, the money is placed so that the quesited
cannot withdraw it.   If the two significators are going
to a □ or ☍, then the attempt to borrow will give
offence, and the parties will quarrel, but if there be
" mutual reception," yet the lord of the quesited's
wealth be weak, he will be willing, but unable to
lend it.

5. *Shall I receive my wages ?*—Take the lords of the
1st and 2nd for the querent, and the 10th and 11th
for the wages and the party who owes them. The
lord of the 1st or 2nd in the 11th, and in good aspect
to the lord of the 10th or 11th, or the ☽ in good
aspect to these lords, the wages will be obtained.   If
the rulers of the 10th and 11th are infortunes, and the
lord of the 1st be in good aspect, then the querent will
obtain his wages after waiting some time ; but if you
find none of these testimonies, but evil aspects between
the lords of the 1st, 2nd, and 10th, or 11th, the
querent will not get them.   The *time* of getting the
money must be judged by the number of degrees the
significators lack in making perfect aspects. (See
" Measure of Time " in Part I.)

6. *Of Bills and Promissory Notes.*—Judge of these
in precisely the same way as for money lent or owing,
in Question 3.

7. *Can I obtain more wages ?*—If you find the lord
of the 2nd favourably aspected and received by the
lord of the 10th or 11th, you can ; also if the ruler of
the 1st or 2nd be in the 11th and not afflicted, and in
" mutual reception " with the lord of the 11th ; but
if there be no aspect or reception between these lords

you will not get advanced, and should the lords of
10th and 11th afflict the lords of 1st and 2nd, better
not ask as it will give offence, and may lead to
dismissal.

8. *Is it well to lend money ?*—If the ruler of the 2nd
be afflicted by the malefics, ℞, or combust, or in bad
aspect to the borrower's significator, then do not lend
it, or if you find his rulers afflicted, and also going to
affliction, do not lend it, for such shows bankruptcy ;
but if you find the lord of his 2nd strong, or applying
to the favourable planets, swift in motion, and
angular, you *may* lend.

CHAPTER III

OF QUESTIONS RELATING TO THE THIRD HOUSE

1. *Shall I agree with my brethren or neighbours ?*—
If the enquiry be about a particular brother, you must
take the house ruling that brother, as the 3rd for the
first brother, the 5th for the second, the 7th for the
third brother, and so on. But if it be respecting
brethren *generally*, or neighbours, then have regard
to the 3rd house, and if you find the ruler a benevolent
planet, or a benevolent planet in the third, and its
lord in good aspect or mutual reception with your
significator, then you will agree, and there will be no
serious differences arise between you. Also, if lord
of 1st be in the 3rd, and lord of 3rd in 1st, and in ✶,
it argues a good understanding, or friendship with
your neighbours and brethren. Also, if the ☽ aspects
favourably the lord of the 3rd, or a planet in the 3rd,
it is a favourable sign.

But if you find the aforesaid significators in ☐, or
the lord of 3rd an evil planet, and afflicting the ☽,
then there will be constant quarrelling ; and if the
evil be by ☍ aspect, then great enmity will exist,
probably law. If the lord of the 3rd be an evil planet,

or an evil planet be in the 3rd, then it is best for the querent to have nothing to do with his brethren or neighbours, and avoid them, for there will be no agreement or harmony between them.

2. *Is it well to go a short journey ?*—The lord of the 1st in the 3rd, and the ☽ in good aspect—or if the lords of 3rd and 1st be swift in motion, and angular, and not afflicted by the malefics, you will go, and succeed ; the lords of 3rd and 1st in good aspects, and not afflicted by the evil planets, a good sign for success, and that you will go. If you find ♃ or ♀ in the 3rd, and ☽ in good aspect, the journey will be pleasant ; the same if the ☽ be there in favourable aspect of ♃, ♀, or lord of the ascendant.

But if you find ♅, ♄, or ♂ in the 3rd, your journey will profit you little ; and if they are afflicting the lord of 1st or ☽, you will suffer through it, and it will be best not to go. Again, if you find the lord of the 1st, 3rd, or the ☽ afflicted by the malefics, best not to go. Mars denotes accidents, hurts, and dangers ; ♄ sickness, delay in reaching your destination ; and ♅ shows unexpected dangers and troubles. If the cusps of the 1st and 3rd are " fixed," or the lord of the 1st or 3rd, ℞, slow in motion, or stationary, then the journey will be delayed, or not come off. The house from which the evil comes shows the difficulty—as if the lord of the 2nd afflicts, money will stop the journey ; if the lord of the 6th, it will be sickness, the lord of the 10th, business, and so on of the other houses.

3. *When may I go a journey ?*—You may go when the lords of the 1st or 3rd are in good aspect ; or the ☽ in good aspect to the lord of the 3rd, and the day (after the question) on which this happens is the day you should go.

NOTE.—*Journeys signified by the 3rd house are short ones, on foot, by cart, or rail ; for long journeys the 9th house must be consulted.*

4. *Is the report true or false, and how will it affect*

me ?—The ☽ in the ascendant, 3rd, 10th, or 11th separating from a good *aspect*, and applying by a good aspect to the lord of the ascendant, then the rumour or report is true, and will benefit the querent. If the ☽ be void, of course it is false ; the same if ☽ and ☿ are afflicting each other by ☐ or ☍. If you find ♄, ♅, or ♂ in the 3rd, the report is of a damaging nature, the same if they afflict the lord of the 3rd ; but if ♃ or ♀ be there, or aspects the lord of the ascendant, then the news or rumour is favourable to the querent.   If the report be ill, and the lord of the ascendant weak and afflicted, the querent will be damaged through it ; or if the lord of the 3rd be in the 1st afflicted, the querent will suffer detriment ; but the lord of the ascendant strong, and angular, and especially in the 10th, or elevated above the afflicting planets, then no ill will befall the querent through the rumour.

5. *Who raised the report ?*—The situation of the lord of the 3rd will show this ; if in the 3rd by a brother or neighbour, in the 4th a father, the 5th some very young person, or a child, the 6th a servant, labourers, or a low and poor person, and so on of the other houses.   You will also judge of anonymous letters by the same rules, and the sign and house occupied by the lord of the 3rd will show the dress, appearance, and station in life of the sender of the letter.

CHAPTER IV

OF QUESTIONS RELATING TO THE FOURTH HOUSE

1. *May I purchase property ?*—If you find ♀ or ♃ in the 2nd or 4th, and in ✶ or △ to the lord of the ascendant, and not afflicted, and the lord of the 4th well placed, either by position or aspect, you may purchase it ; but if you find none of these testimonies, and the lord of the 4th weak, or afflicting the lord of

the 1st or 2nd, or an infortune in the 1st, 2nd, or 4th, do not make the purchase.

2. *Can I purchase the property ?*—If you find the lord of the 7th and lord of the 1st in ☌ or good aspect, and without *frustration*, or if there be *translation of light between* these lords, you can purchase.   If there be reception between these lords, and they be in ▢ to each other, you can purchase, but there will be much delay and suspicion in the matter.   But should there be no *reception*, or *aspect*, or *translation* between these lords, or if they be in ▢ or ☍, and the infortunes occupy the 7th, 10th, or 4th, you will not agree.

If you find ♄, ♅, or ♂ in the 7th or 2nd, and he not lord of that house, be wary of the purchase, for it will do you harm ; if the lord of the 7th be in the 1st or 2nd, it is a bad sign, but the lord of the 1st in the 7th or 8th is favourable.

3. *Will it be dear or cheap ?*—The lord of the 10th *angular* and strong, the price will be high ; but if cadent, weak, or afflicted, it will be low.

4. *What is the quality of the property ?*—This is shown by the 4th house and its lord, if the infortunes occupy this house, or its lord be cadent and weak, the property is not good ; but if the fortunes occupy this house, and its lord be strong and angular, it is good, and worth the money.   The lord of the 10th strong, direct, and swift in motion, the property will let well ; but if weak, ℞, or cadent, it will not let, but be a heavy burden to the querent.

Respecting *land*, if ♈, ♌, or ♐ be on the cusp of the 4th, or its lord occupy these signs, it will be high, dry, stony, hilly, and barren.   If ♉, ♍, or ♑, it will be arable land, a mixed soil, capable of good cultivation ; if ♋, ♏ , or ♓, it will be wet, lay low, and be sometimes flooded ; if ♊, ♎, and ♒, there will be much wood.

5. *Whether treasure be concealed in the ground ?*—If the lord of the 4th be in the 4th, there is treasure, and

the nature of this planet will show the nature of the treasure. ♄ denotes lead and coal ; ♂ ironstone, flints, granite, etc. ; ♃ silver or tin ; the ☉ gold or jewels ; ♀ copper ; ☿ silver, or ornaments, money, books, and medals ; the ☽ silver. If the lord of the 4th be in his house or exaltation, there is treasure ; but if otherwise, judge there is none, and especially if this lord be weak, cadent, or afflicted. If you find signs of treasure in the figure, and the lord of the 4th applies to a good aspect of lord of 2nd, or the lord of the 2nd applies to the lord of the 4th, you will obtain the treasure, and you should seek it on the day these lords meet in good aspect.

6. *Shall I remove ?*—If moveable signs occupy the 1st and 7th cusps, or if the lords of these houses, or the ☽ be in moveable signs, you are sure to remove. But if the angles and their rulers be in *fixed* signs, and the ☽ slow in motion, or in the beginning or middle of a sign, you will not remove.

7. *Is it well to remove ?*—The lord of the 7th better aspected or better placed than the lord of the 1st, or evil planets in the 1st, 2nd, or 4th, or the lord of the 1st or ☽ separating from the malefics, it is best to remove ; but if the 7th house or its lord be afflicted, or the lord of the 10th, or that house be afflicted more than the lords of the 1st or 4th, then it is better to remain ; it is also better to remain if the lord of the 1st be in the 1st or 4th, and strong. In short, take the 1st and 4th and their lords for your present abode, and the 7th and 10th and their lords for your removal, and whichever is the strongest of the two will show whether you should remove or not.

8. *When shall I remove ?*—See when the lord of the 1st or 7th leaves the sign he is then in, and about that time the querent will remove.

9. *Am I likely to suffer by my removal, if so, in what way ?*—Have regard to the lord of the 7th, and see by what planet he is afflicted ; if by lord of 8th then it will be money ; if lord of 9th, brethren or friends ;

lord of 10th, the father, or the house will not be suit-
able ; if the lord of the 11th, children will oppose or
interfere ; if the lord of the 12th, sickness, bad
servants, etc. ; if lord of 1st, enemies, lawsuits, wife
opposes ; if lord of 2nd, danger of sudden death ; if
lord of 3rd, by means of wife's kindred ; if lord of
4th, honour, credit, or trade will suffer ; if lord of
5th, false friends ; if lord of 6th, secret persecution
from private enemies.   Take the 7th house as the 1st,
and reckon the other houses accordingly as shown.

10. *Shall I inherit my father's property ?*—If there
be good agreement between the lords of the 2nd and
5th, or if the ☽ be separating from the lord of 5th, and
applying to the lord of 2nd, you will inherit it ; the
same if the lord of 1st disposes of the lord of 5th ; also
if ♃ or ♀ be in the 5th, in good aspect to the lord of
the 2nd ; but if you find the lords of 1st and 4th in
bad aspect or without reception, and the lord of 1st
afflicted, it is doubtful.   See what planet afflicts the
lord of 1st, and from that quarter the querent will
meet trouble.

11. *To find anything hidden or mislaid.*—If it
belongs to the querent, take the 2nd house ; if to his
brother, the 4th ; his child, the 6th ; his wife, the
8th, etc. ; if the lord of the 2nd (as described above)
be in an angle, it is in the house of the owner, and if
the lord of the 2nd be in the ascendant, it is in that
part of the house wherein he mostly abides, but if
this lord be in the 10th, it is in the hall or dining-room ;
but if the querent be a mechanic or tradesman it is
in his shop ; if the lord of the 2nd be in the 7th, it is
where his wife mostly works.   If a fortune be rising,
or the lord of the 2nd be in the ascendant, it will be
found again, the same if the lord of 1st be in the 2nd,
or the ☽ in trine to the lord of the 2nd, or the lord of
the 4th in good aspect to the lord of the 1st or 2nd,
and well dignified.   A favourable sign are the lights
above the earth, the missing articles are almost sure
to be then found ; but if you find them under the

earth, and the lord of the 2nd afflicted, the articles will not be found or recovered.

The *quality* of the place where the article is, may be known by the sign the significators are in, and the sign on the cusp of the 2nd. If these be *airy* it is hidden in the topmost part of the house, or the eaves, or the top of the room in which it is. If *watery* it is near the wash-house, sink, pool, river ; in *fiery* signs, near the chimney or fire, near iron; if in *earthy* signs it is near, or in, the ground or floor. If the significator be going out of one sign into another, it is behind something, or fallen down between two rooms, or near a door or threshold joining two rooms.

NOTE.—If the lord of the 2nd be in a succeedent house it is out of the house and in the garden, yard, or out-buildings, not far distant from the house, but if this lord be cadent it is far away, or lost or hid at some distance. Judge of the *locality, direction,* etc., it is in, by the *nature* and quality of the signs occupying the cusp of the 2nd, and containing the significator, and which you will find explained in Part I.

The nature of the article mislaid can be judged by the ruler of the 2nd, or *planet therein.* ♄ shows lead, iron, tin instruments, black cloths, boots, leather, agricultural implements, umbrellas, carts, etc ; ♃, oil, paint, men's clothes, poultry, silk, honey, money, or any kind of merchandise ; ♂ shows arms, brass, knives, cutlery, swords, and all sharp or cutting instruments ; ☉, gold, jewels, and valuable articles ; ♀, women's clothes, rings, brooches, and ornaments ; ☿, paper, or paper money, deeds, books, letters, scientific instruments, etc. ; ☽, all common things as crockery, china, saucepans, kettles, brushes, and such things as are in every-day use ; ♅, models, machinery, galvanic apparatus and all uncommon *novelties.*

A great deal of practice or experience is required before you can answer questions of this nature satisfactorily, because there are thousands of different articles, there are thousands of places in which they may be lost or hid, and there are dozens of different directions in which they may be, hence this is one of the most difficult questions in Horary Astrology. I advise the young student not to go further AT FIRST *than judging if the article will be recovered, and if so, let him ascertain where it actually was, and compare the place and direction with the figure. A little experience this way will instruct him more than all the printed books in the world.*

CHAPTER V

OF QUESTIONS RELATING TO THE FIFTH HOUSE

1. *Shall I have any family or not ?*—Have regard to the ascendant and 5th house, and if the signs occupying those be *fruitful*, or their lords be in fruitful signs, or ☽, ♀, or ♃ be in the 5th, you may judge in the affirmative ; if ♉ or ♐ occupies the cusp of the 5th, and the ☽ be in a fruitful sign, and in aspect to the lord of the 5th, any planet in the 5th, in favourable aspect to the ☽, ♀, or ♃, a very small family ; but if ☽, ♃, or ♀, be there in fruitful or bicorporeal signs (especially ♓), a large family is signified ; if these planets receive afflictions from the evil planets some of the offspring will die ; if a malefic occupies the 5th house in a fruitful sign, and is afflicted, there will be several born, but they will all perish. ♂ is particularly evil this way, and his ☐ or ☍ to a planet in the 5th denotes sudden death to the offspring ; but if you find a barren sign on the cusp of the 5th, or an infortune in any sign but a fruitful, it denotes no family. ♈, ♌, ♍, ♑, and ♒ are against a family, and if the lord of any of these signs be in another of them, as ♈ on 5th, and ♂ lord of it in ♌, then it is a testimony of no family. The number of children depends on the testimonies that exist, the fortunes in good aspect in the 5th in ♓, give a very large

family, probably over a dozen ; if in ♋, less, about
9 ; if in ♏, less still, about 6 ; in ♎ and ♐ from 4 to
6. The best way is, to put down the testimonies *for*
and *against*, and according to the majority of testimonies decide the number of the family.

  2. *A female inquires if she may become encéinte.*—
The lord of the 1st in the 5th or 7th, or the lord of the
5th in a fruitful sign, or a fruitful sign occupying the
6th, she will conceive ; but if you find these rules
in barren signs, and these signs occupy the cusps of
the 1st and 5th, and the lord of the 5th afflicted, she
will not conceive. The ☽ badly situated is a sign of
barrenness.

  3. *A woman asks at what time she may become
encéinte.*—If you find that she will have offspring,
then look to the lord of the 5th, if you find him in the
1st house judge the first year ; if in the 2nd, the second
year ; in the 10th, the third year; the 7th, the fourth
year ; if in the 4th, the fifth year ; and if this lord be
swift in motion, and in a moveable sign, it accelerates
it, but if cadent, ℞, or in fixed signs, it delays it.

  4. *A woman asks if she be encéinte or not.*—If the
lord of the ascendant, or ☽, aspects the lord of the 5th
from angles and fruitful signs, it is so ; if ♃, ☽, or ♀ not
afflicted in the 5th, and in signs that give children, it
is so ; but if these planets be afflicted by the malefics,
she will miscarry, or the child will be still-born ; ♃
or ♀ in the 7th, in fruitful signs, is a good testimony,
and the ☽ in an angle, in a fruitful sign, leaving a good
aspect of the 5th, she has just conceived. But if
you find the lord of the 5th in ♊, ♌, or ♍, or the
malefics in the 5th, then judge she is not unless
the malefics be in fruitful signs when she will either
miscarry or have a still-born.

  5. *Whether the child will be male or female.*—If the
lord of the 5th be in a masculine sign, and a masculine
sign be on the cusp of the 5th, it will be a boy ; the
same if the *majority* of the significators are in masculine signs, and the ☽ applies to a masculine planet ;

but if these lords and houses be feminine ; or ♀ or ☽ in the 5th, it will be a girl. ♅, ♄, ♃, ♂, and ☉ denote boys ; the ☽ and ♀ girls. If you find the majority of planets in double-bodied signs (♊, ♐, or ♓), and ♃, ♀, or ☽ well aspected in the 5th, then judge there will be *twins.*

6. *Will the child live or die ?*—If you find the lord of the 5th cadent, weak, and afflicted, or the malefics in the 5th, and not in favourable aspect to the ☽, ♃, or ♀, it will die ; if these testimonies do not exist, and the lord of the 5th be strong and angular, unafflicted, or ☽, ♀, or ♃ in the 5th, the child will live ; but if any of the infortunes be heavily afflicted in the 5th, it will be born alive, but perish afterwards.

NOTE.—If a man asks any of these questions, take the 7th and 11th, and judge exactly as explained, reckoning the 7th as the 1st and the 11th as the 5th.

7. *Is the female chaste ?*—The lords of the 1st and 5th in fixed signs, and fixed signs on these houses and many planets angular, she is chaste and honest. ♃ in the 5th, a good sign; also if the ☽ be angular and fixed; but ♅, ♄, or ♂ afflicting the ☽ or ♀, or in the 5th or 11th, or the ☽ or ♀ in the 5th or 11th, and afflicted by ♂ or ♅ afflicting the ☉ or ♀ in any house or sign, and a moveable sign be on the 5th, then judge she is not, and that she has given way to temptation.   The aspect or position of ♅ is almost a sure sign.

8. *A child lost or absconded.—Will it return or be found ?*—The lords of the 1st and 5th going to a ☌ or good aspect, it returns or is found ; if to a bad aspect the parent will hear of it ; the lord of the 5th turning ℞, it will return.   The ☽ translating light from the lord of the 5th to the 1st, it will be heard of or found ; but if the lord of the 5th be cadent, and in no aspect to the lord of the 1st, and there be no translation of light between the two significators, the child will not return or be found.   All the significators under the Earth, a bad sign ; if above, a

good sign. If the child has absconded, and the lord of the 5th be cadent, swift in motion, and in a moveable sign, it will never return or be found. The *direction* the child is gone, its distance from home, and its condition must be judged from the location of the lord of the 5th, and in a similar way to that shown in Chapter IV, Question 11.

9. *Of horse, foot, or boat-racing. Shall I gain by backing this horse, man, or boat?*—Much difficulty is often experienced in matters of this kind, and the books published are mostly mute on these subjects, but note the following. If you find the lord of the 1st, 2nd, or 5th on the midheaven, it is almost a sure sign of gain, and in my experience it has never failed ; the lord of the 5th in the 5th, and in good aspect to the lord of the 1st or 2nd, a favourable sign. ♃ strong in the 5th or 2nd, the lord of 5th *angular* and free from affliction, a good sign ; but unless you find some of these testimonies it will not be safe to speculate in the betting ; or if you find the lord of the 11th, or the 11th house stronger than the 5th, or its lord, the horse, man, or boat will not win.

10. *Of lotteries and prizes. Shall I win a prize?*— Lords of the 1st, 2nd, and 5th, strong, angular, and in good aspect, you will safely win ; or if these planets be strong, and the ☽ translates the light from the lord of the 5th to the lord of the 2nd, it is a good testimony. The lord of the 5th or 2nd on the midheaven and strong, or the majority of planets *angular*, you will win ; but if the lord of the 1st, 2nd, or 5th be afflicted in any way, or the lord of the 5th in the 2nd, you will lose, and your ticket prove a blank.

With respect to raffles, cards, etc., judge similar to above. If you find your significator *angular*, strong, and in elevation above all the other planets, and in his own house, it is favourable ; but to be *sure* of winning in these hazardous games, it is necessary for the lords of the 1st and 2nd to be in their own houses, *angular,* in elevation, and absolutely free from evil aspect.

CHAPTER VI

OF QUESTIONS RELATING TO THE SIXTH HOUSE

1. *May I deal in small cattle ?*—By *small* cattle are meant sheep, pigs, goats ; also dogs, cats, and all animals smaller than a donkey.

If you find a malefic in the 6th, or the lord of the 6th afflicting the lord of the 1st, 2nd, or 4th, or the lord of the 6th weak, retrograde, cadent, and afflicted, it will be best to leave them alone ; but if you find a fortune in the 6th, or the ☉ or ☽ well aspected in the 6th, and in good aspect to the lord of the 1st or 2nd, or both ; or the lord of the 6th strong, angular, and in favourable aspect to the lord of the 1st or 2nd, you may deal in them, and will benefit thereby.

2. *When may I buy ?*—Observe when the lord of the 6th is in favourable aspect to the lord of the 1st ; and if at that time the ☽ *separating* from the malefics, and *applying* to the benefics by ☌, or *good aspect*, it will be the most favourable time the querent can choose ; but never buy when the ☽ is leaving the benefics and applying to the infortunes.

3. *When may I sell ?*—The best time to sell is when the ☽, or lord of the 6th, is separating from the benefic planets, and applying to the infortunes ; observe the day on which this happens, and on that day the querent should sell.

4. *Of lost cattle, and runaway servants.*—If the lord of the 6th be ℞, or if it forms a good aspect to the lord of the 1st, or if there be translation of light from the lord of the 6th to the lord of the 1st, the lost one will return ; but if you find the lord of the 6th swift and cadent, especially in the 3rd and 9th, and there be no reception, translation, or good aspect between the lords of the 1st and 6th ; or if the lord of this house be in □, or ☍, to the lord of the 1st, the cattle

or servant will not return. The locality and direction of the lord of the 6th will show the direction and place where the strayed one is.

5. *Is my servant honest ?*—The lord of the 6th in good aspect to the lord of the 1st ; or ♃ or ♀, in the 6th, or the ☽ there in good aspect of ♃ or ♀, then judge the servant is honest ; but if you find an infortune in the 6th or ☿ there, in ♍, ♈, or ♑, or in any other sign *afflicted*, and ♃ in no benevolent aspect, the servant or labourer is dishonest, and will not benefit the querent, or do justice ; the ☽ in the 6th, afflicted by ♂ or ♄, the servant is not to be trusted.

6. *May I engage this servant ?*—Judge as above ; and if this map is favourable, then engage the servant on that day that the ☽, or lord of the ascendant, forms a good aspect, or ☌, with the lord of the 6th house.

7. *Will my tenant stay or remove ?*—The cusps of the 6th or 12th fixed, or their lords in fixed signs, he will not go ; but if moveable signs occupy these cusps, or their lords be in moveable signs, or about to change signs, the tenant will remove. Judge this question *exactly* as for *removals* in chapter 4, reckoning the 6th house as the 1st, and the 12th as the 7th, etc.

OF SICKNESS

8. *What part of the body is afflicted ?*—Have regard to the 6th house, and see what sign is on its cusp, in what sign its lord is, and what planets (if any) are in the 6th ; the parts shown by the place of the ☽, and the lord of the ascendant, will also suffer. For instance, in figure 2, we find ♓ on the cusp of the 6th, the ☉ in the 6th in ♈, ♃, its lord, in ♊, and the ☽ in ♎, and the lord of the ascendant in ♒; ♃, lord of the 6th, and ruling the liver, denotes that it is deranged, and being in ♊, pleurisy and pains in the shoulders (ruled by ♊), cold, clammy feet (ruled by ♓) ; but the head hot, and the system inclined to be ever ish (☉ in ♈ ruling the head, and a hot planet) ;

☽ in ♎ some pain in the lower part of the back, about the reins, and across the loins ; and ♀, ruler of the 1st, in ♒, denotes the legs and ankles, a touch of gout, or swelling in those parts.

9. *Will it be a long sickness or short ?*—The ☽, and lord of the 1st and 6th in *moveable* signs, swift in motion, denote a short sickness ; or if the lord of 1st and 6th are going to a good aspect, it is a favourable sign ; but if you find these rulers in *fixed* signs, or ♄ in the 6th, then you may fear a long illness ; but where you find the significators in common signs, it will not be very long, or very short ; the lords of 1st and 6th in affliction, or afflicting each other, denote a severe illness ; and if ♅ be the afflicting planet, it will never be cured ; the lord of the 1st in the 6th afflicted, and ℞, denotes a tedious sickness, and very severe.

10. *When shall I recover ?*—Have regard to the lords of the 1st and 6th and the ☽, and when these meet in favourable aspect you will recover, according to the " measure of time," stated in *Part I*. For instance, in figure No. 2, ♀ lady of 1st is going to △ of ♃ lord of the 6th ; ♀ in an angle in fixed signs denotes *months* and she lacks a little over 3° of a △, hence in rather more than 3 months he would recover. The ☽ is angular and moveable, and is 5° off a △ of ♀, would signify that in 5 days a change would occur for the better, and again in 3 days after that, when she meets the △ of ♃.

11. *Is the sickness dangerous ?*—If you find the lord of the ascendant strong, and not in the 4th, 6th, or 8th, and especially if assisted by a good influence of ♃, and the ☽ be also well placed, there is no danger ; the ☽ in a moveable or common sign, not in the 8th, and not afflicted by the lord of the 8th, there is no danger ; if the lord of the 1st disposes of the lord of the 8th, and be in ✶ or △ to ♃, ♀, ☉ or ☽ there is no danger ; but if you find the lord of the ascendant or the ☽ going to the ☌ of lord of 8th, and in the 4th, 6th,

or 8th, or if the lord of the 1st be going to combustion, or to the □ or ☍ of ♂ or ♄, and from the 4th, 6th, or 8th, it is very bad, and threatens death. The malefics in the 4th, 6th, 8th, or 12th, violently afflicting the ☉ or ☽, show danger, and unless ♃ or ♀ intervenes with a friendly aspect, the sick will die.

12. *The doctor and physic.*—If the lord of the 7th (which shows the doctor) be afflicting the lord of the 1st or ☽, he will not *cure* the patient ; and if the lord of the 10th (the physic) afflicts in a similar way, the medicine is doing harm ; if the 7th lord is friendly, and the lord of the 10th is not so, the doctor will ultimately cure by changing the physic, and *vice versa*, the physic will cure, or do good, but the presence of the doctor will be distasteful to the patient.

CHAPTER VII

THE DISEASES SHOWN BY THE PLANETS IN THE DIFFERENT SIGNS

Diseases of Herschel

♅ may be judged in all the signs the same as ♄, only bear in mind that whatever disease he signifies it will never be cured.

Diseases of Saturn

♄ in ♈ signifies rheum, melancholy vapours, cold in the head, obstructions, stoppage in the stomach, pains in the teeth, deafness, etc.

♄ in ♉ swelling in the neck and throat, king's evil, scurvy, hoarseness, melancholy, and chronic distempers about the neck and throat.

♄ in ♊ signifies infirmities incident to the arms and shoulders, consumption, black jaundice, and diseases proceeding from bad blood.

♄ in ♋ denotes phthisis, ulcerations in the lungs, obstructions and bruises in the breast, ague, scurvy, cancer, etc.

♄ in ♌ signifies the heart afflicted by grief or poison, consumption of the reins or inward parts, vapours, weakness, and pains in the back.

♄ in ♍ shows the blood corrupted, obstructions in the bowels, costiveness, weakness in the thighs, melancholy, gripings, stone, etc.

♄ in ♎ shows the blood corrupted, back and kidneys distempered, strangury pains in the knees and thighs, sciatica and gout.

♄ in ♏ denotes swellings or distempers of the secret parts, melancholy, piles, palsy, gout in the hands and feet.

♄ in ♐ signifies weakness in the hips and thighs, old aches and bruises in those parts, and sciatica or gout.

♄ in ♑ denotes the gout in the lower parts, pains and obstructions in the head, ague, etc.

♄ in ♒ signifies disorders in the head and teeth, defects in the ears, pains in the joints, bruises, swellings in the legs, and sometimes a sore throat.

♄ in ♓ gives defluxions of rheums, king's evil, consumption, all distempers of the feet and toes, such as the gout and illness by colds.

Diseases of Jupiter

♃ in ♈ produces distempers in the head, a quinsy or swelling in the throat, chiefly from ill blood in the veins of the head, and causes strange dreams and imaginations.

♃ in ♉ brings distempers in the throat, wind in the blood, gripings in the bowels, and goutish humours in the hands and arms.

♃ in ♊.—A pleurisy or some disorders of the reins.

♃ in ♋ gives the dropsy, the stomach offended, bad appetite, corrupt blood, scurvy, surfeits, etc.

♃ in ♌ indicates fevers, pleurisy, the heart ill affected.

♃ in ♍ indicates a consumpton, obstructions of the lungs, melancholy, cold and dry liver.

♃ in ♎ shows the patient hath too much blood, whence arise obstructions, corrupt blood, fevers, piles, tumours, inflammations etc.

♃ in ♏ signifies the strangury, piles, the blood surcharged with watery humours, whence arise dropsy, etc.

♃ in ♐ denotes some choleric distemper, arising from putrefaction of the blood ; a fever, pains and swellings about the knees, etc.

♃ in ♑.—The patient is afflicted with melancholy, obstructions in the throat, etc.

♃ in ♒.—The blood abounds too much, whence it is corrupted, and many diseases and flying pains afflict the body. It gives lumbago.

♃ in ♓.—The blood is too thin and watery, which breeds dropsy.

Diseases of Mars.

♂ in ♈ signifies the patient is almost distracted with a pain in his head, rheum in the eyes, want of rest, etc.

♂ in ♉ denotes extreme pains in the throat and neck, king's evil, weakness in the loins, and the gravel or stone.

♂ in ♊ shows the blood is corrupted ; itch, breakings out, surfeits, fevers, pains in the arms and shoulders, disorders in the secret parts, strangury, etc.

♂ in ♋ indicates pains in the breast and stomach, a dry cough, or a tumour in the thighs, accidents to the feet.

♂ in ♌ denotes affliction at the heart, choleric humours, gravel in the kidneys, pain in the knees, etc.

♂ in ♍ signifies choleric humours, obstructions in the bowels, bloody flux, worms in children, humours in the legs.

♂ in ♎ produces diseases in the reins and kidneys, stone or gravel, urine hot, lues, etc., as may be suspected.

♂ in ♏ shows suspicion of some venereal distemper, or ulcer in the secret parts, pains in the bladder, pains in the head, overflowing of courses, etc.

♂ in ♐ produces pain or ulcers in the hips and thighs by humours settled in those parts, and an extreme heat in the mouth and throat.

♂ in ♑ denotes lameness in the knees, hands, or arms, or a flying gout.

♂ in ♒ signifies blood overheated, pains in the legs, surfeit or fever.

♂ in ♓ gives lameness in the feet, by corrupt humours settled there ; sometimes the heart is afflicted, etc.

Diseases of the Sun

☉ in ♈ produces sore eyes, megrims, head disturbed, fevers, etc.

☉ in ♉ denotes tumours in the knees, quinsy or sore throat, breakings out, and swellings in those parts.

☉ in ♊.—Blood inflamed, pestilential fevers, breakings out in several parts of the body, scurvy, pains and weakness in the legs.

☉ in ♋ shows the measles or small-pox, a disordered stomach, hoarseness, dropsy or swelling in the feet.

☉ in ♌ indicates violent pains in the head, madness, stone, pains in the back, plague, spotted fever,

⊙ in ♍ produces humours in the bowels, obstruction in the stomach, bloody flux, sore throat, or swellings in the neck.

⊙ in ♎.—Inflammation of the blood, pains in the arms and shoulders, stone and gravel, the venereal distemper, etc.

⊙ in ♏ indicates distempers in the secret parts, sharpness of urine, obstructions of the stomach and female courses.

⊙ in ♐.—The thighs are afflicted by hot humours, a fistula, fever, swoonings, etc.

⊙ in ♑ signifies lameness about the knees, bowels disordered, and a fever.

⊙ in ♒.—The blood inflamed, breakings out, reins disordered, gravel, stone, strangury.

⊙ in ♓.—The secret parts afflicted, strangury, and violent pains in those parts.

Diseases of Venus

♀ in ♈ indicates the disease is in the head from abundance of moist humours, lethargy, reins afflicted, and head disordered by cold.

♀ in ♉ signifies pains in the head or secret parts, swellings in the neck from moist humours in the head.

♀ in ♊ denotes a corrupted blood, king's evil, dropsy, and a flux of rheum.

♀ in ♋ shows the stomach is much offended with cold, raw, undigested humours, many times with a surfeit, etc.

♀ in ♌.— Some ill affection of the heart, love passion, etc. ; pains in the legs, of bad consequence.

♀ in ♍ shows some distemper in the bowels, the flux, or the worms, mucus in the bowels.

♀ in ♎ denotes a gonorrhoea or distemper in the reins, or surfeit by too plentiful eating or drinking, and windy disorders.

7

♀ in ♏ produces some venereal distemper, and pain in the private parts, etc.

♀ in ♐.—Hip gout, surfeit, cold and moist humours.

♀ in ♑ produces gout in the knees and thighs, and swellings in those parts.

♀ in ♒.—Pain and swellings in the legs or knees from a cold cause, and the heart afflicted.

♀ in ♓ indicates lameness in the feet, swellings in the legs, a flux, windy complaints.

Diseases of Mercury.

☿ in ♈ shows the disease lies in the head and brain, vertigo and spasms in the head, and sometimes disorders of the womb.

☿ in ♉ produces defects in the throat, swellings in the neck, hoarseness, and also pain in the feet.

☿ in ♊ signifies windiness in the blood, gouty pains in the head, arms, etc.

☿ in ♋ produces a cold stomach, gripings, windiness, distillation of rheum, lameness in the legs and knees from colds, etc.

☿ in ♌ indicates tremblings, melancholy, pains in the back, occasioned by colds caught in the feet.

☿ in ♍ imports much wind in the bowels, obstructions, pains in the head, short breath, and wind cholic.

☿ in ♎ shows stoppage of urine, obstructions, blood disordered, breast, lungs, and reins afflicted.

☿ in ♏ denotes distempers in the secret parts, afflictions of the bowels, running pains in the arms and shoulders.

☿ in ♐ shows distempers in the reins, weakness in the back, stoppage at the stomach, coughs, swellings in the hips and thighs.

☿ in ♑ denotes stoppage of urine, goutish humours above the knees, pains in the back, melancholy, etc.

☿ in ♒ imports wind in the blood, running pains in different parts of the body, fluxes and disorders in the bowels.

☿ in ♓ signifies pains in the head, weakness in the legs and feet, a gonorrhœa, or a distemper in the reins, etc.

Diseases of the Moon

☽ in ♈ signifies convulsions, defluxions of rheum from the head, lethargy, weakness in the eyes, and pains in the knees.

☽ in ♉ produces pains in the legs and feet, swellings, stoppage in and sore throat, etc.

☽ in ♊ denotes a wandering gout in the legs, arms hands and feet, surfeits and great obstructions.

☽ in ♋ shows the stomach much afflicted, a surfeit, small-pox, convulsions, falling sickness, tympany, or dropsy.

☽ in ♌.— The heart afflicted, sore throat, quinsy, king's evil, etc.

☽ in ♍ signifies great pain and disorders in the bowels, melancholy blood, obstructions, weakness in the arms and shoulders.

☽ in ♎ denotes the reins are distempered, obstructions in the stomach, weakness in the back, surfeits, pleurisy.

☽ in ♏ shows the distemper is in the secrets, small-pox, dropsy, poison, the heart afflicted, swoonings.

☽ in ♐ imports lameness or weakness in the thighs, distempers in the bowels, etc.

☽ in ♑ signifies the stone, weak back, gout in the knees, etc.

☽ in ♒ signifies hysterics, swellings and pains in the legs and secret parts.

☽ in ♓ shows cold taken in the feet, and body disordered thereby, swellings in the legs, dropsies, and the body overcharged with moist humours.

A TABLE

SHOWING WHAT PARTS OF MAN'S BODY EVERY PLANET SIGNIFIES IN THE TWELVE SIGNS

Sign	♄	♃	♂	☉	♀	☿	☽
♈	head breast arms	head throat heart	head bowels eyes	thighs head	reins feet head	secrets legs	knees head
♉	heart breast throat	shoulders belly throat	reins throat neck	knees throat	secrets neck throat	thighs feet	legs throat
♊	belly heart arms	breast reins arms	secrets arms shoulders	legs ankles arms	thighs throat arms	knees head arms	feet shoulders arms
♋	reins belly breast	heart secrets breast	breast stomach thighs	feet breast	arms knees breast	throat legs	head breast stomach
♌	secrets reins heart	thighs belly heart	heart back reins	head heart	breast legs heart	arms shoulders feet	neck throat heart
♍	thighs secrets bowels	knees reins bowels	bowels legs	neck throat bowels	heart back feet	breast head bowels	arms shoulders bowels
♎	knees thighs reins	legs secrets reins	reins feet	arms shoulders reins	head belly reins	heart back throat	breast reins stomach
♏	legs feet secrets	feet thighs secrets	secrets head	breast stomach secrets	reins throat secrets	belly arms shoulders	secrets heart back
♐	feet legs thighs	head knees thighs	thighs neck throat	heart back thighs	secrets shoulders thighs	reins breast stomach	bowels thighs guts
♑	head feet knees	neck legs knees	knees arms shoulders	bowels guts knees	thighs breasts knees	secrets heart back	reins knees
♒	neck head thighs	arms shoulders legs	legs breast stomach	reins legs	knees heart legs	thighs bowels guts	secrets legs
♓	arms neck feet	breast head feet	feet heart back	secrets feet	legs belly feet	knees reins	thighs feet

♅ *may be considered the same as* ♄.

CHAPTER VIII

OF QUESTIONS RELATING TO THE SEVENTH HOUSE

PARTNERSHIPS

1. *May I enter into partnership ?*—♃, ♀, or the ☽ in the 7th ; the lord of the 7th in good aspect to the lord of the 1st or 2nd ; the lord of the 1st in the 7th or 8th ; translation of light between the lords of the 1st and 7th or 8th ; or these lords in mutual reception, you *may* join ; but if you find ♅, ♄, ♂, or even ☿ (if in ♑ or ♏), or the lord of the 7th in the 2nd, or afflicting the lord of the 1st or 2nd ; or the lord of the 7th *afflicted* by the malefics, or the lord of the 8th afflicted, the querent had better *not* join.

2. *How shall we agree ?*—If the lords of the 1st and 7th be in *fixed* signs, or *one* in a fixed and the *other* in a common sign, you *will* agree ; but if both significators be in *moveable* signs, or one in a *common* and the other in a *moveable*, you will not agree, but there will be constant quarrelling. If one significator be in a fixed sign and the other in a moveable, there will be quarelling, but not such as will lead to a dissolution.

3. *About what shall we quarrel ?*—If you find signs of quarrelling, then see if there be a planet afflicting either significator, or the lords of the 2nd or 8th, and if so, that planet and the house it rules will show the matter about which there will be disputes. If the lord of the 10th afflicts, it will be about business generally ; the same if the lord of the 4th afflicts ; if it be the lord of the 3rd or 9th, it will be about the transit of goods, or through letters, and such matters as are ruled by these houses.

4. *Shall we be successful in business ?*—The lord of the 10th and the ☽ in *good* aspect, or *both* strong and angular : ♃, ☉, or ☽ in the 10th, well aspected, you will be very successful ; but if the lord of the 10th be cadent, afflicted, or the ☽ be ill placed, and weak,

and the malefics hold the angles, you will not do well ; and observe well the lord of the 10th and ☽, and the stronger or weaker you find these, the better or worse will be the business or success.

NOTE.—If you find the lord of the 7th or 8th afflicted peregrine, or badly placed, the quesited or partner is in straits for money, and does not know what to do for the best. Never join a partner unless the lords of 7th and 8th be tolerably well placed, and *not afflicted* or *going to affliction,* for such positions denote the man to have heavy liabilities.

OF LAWSUITS

5. *Shall I have law ?*—The lords of the 1st and 7th going to a ☐ or ☍ ; or if you find ♄, ♅, or ♂ in the 7th ; or if there be no *reception, translation of light,* or *collection* between the two significators, and if fixed signs occupy the cusps of the 1st and 7th, you will have law ; but if you find the significators in ⚹ or △, or there be *translation* or *collection,* or the cusps of the 1st or 7th be *moveable* you *will not,* but the dispute may be arranged without law.

6. *Who will be most ready to agree ?*—If you find signs of a settlement without recourse to law, have regard to that planet which *applies* to the other, or *translates* or *collects* the light, and the party signified by the house this planet rules will be the most ready to agree, or who will arrange the dispute. For instance, if lord of 1st applies to lord of 7th, the querent will be most ready to agree, but *vice versa,* the quesited will seek to be reconciled ; if by a planet *translating* or *collecting* the light, and this planet rules the 2nd or 8th, it will be effected through money ; if the 3rd and 9th, through brethren or neighbours ; if the 4th or 10th, fathers, mothers, lands or houses ; the 5th or 11th, by friends ; the 6th or 12th by uncles, aunts, etc.

7. *Who will conquer in a lawsuit ?*—If you find the lord of the 1st stronger than the lord of the 7th, and

not afflicted by the lord of the 10th or 4th, and the lord of the 10th or 7th not in the 1st or 2nd, the querent overcomes ; but if the lord of the 7th be stronger than the lord of the 1st, or be in the 2nd house, and not afflicted by the lords of the 10th or 4th, the adversary gains. The lord of the 1st or 2nd going to combustion, or ♅, ♄, or ♂ in the 7th, afflicting the lord of the 1st, the opponent conquers. If both rulers are strong alike, neither will overcome, but they will be nonsuited ; if lord of 10th afflicts both lords of 1st and 7th, they will both suffer.

8. *Will the judge or lawyer act fairly ?*—♅, ♄, or ♂ in the 10th, he will not act fairly or decide properly ; but ☉, ♃, ♀ there, he will, and may be trusted with the case ; if the lord of the 10th afflict either significator, the judge will be against that party. The lord of the 10th in friendly aspect to both significators, the judge will arrange it fairly and satisfactorily to both parties ; but if the lord of 10th afflict both rulers, neither party will be satisfied with the judge's decision. If ♊ or ♓ holds the cusps of either 1st or 7th, the case will be moved to another court.

OF BUYING AND SELLING

9. *Of buying and selling generally.*—The 1st denotes the person who *wants* to sell or buy, the 7th the party he wants to deal with. If the malefics be in the 7th do not buy ; if they occupy the 1st there will be great labour in the purchase, and much trouble ; if ☽ be *void of course* there will be no bargain ; if she be not void of course, but separates from the malefics, and applies to the benefics, you may buy ; but if she applies to the malefics you may *sell*, but not buy.

PUBLIC ENEMIES

10. *Of public enemies.*—If you find the infortunes in the 7th, he has enemies ; if they be strong by house or exaltation they are *powerful enemies ;* if they

afflict the lord of the 1st or 2nd they will injure the querent, especially if the querent's significators, or the ☽, be disposed by the malefics, and afflicted also ; if the lord of the 7th be an evil planet, and afflicts the lord of the 1st or 2nd, and is not disposed of by the querent's significator, the querent will still suffer damage ; the *number* of enemies can be seen by the evil aspects formed to the lord of the ascendant or the ☽ ; and the houses that these planets are rulers of, which afflict the querent's significator, will show what relation his enemies bear towards him ; if the lord of the 3rd afflicts, then brethren and neighbours are his enemies ; if lord of 4th, very old people ; lord of 5th, young persons ; lord of 6th, servants, labourers, and tenants ; lord of 7th, persons with whom he deals in business ; lord of 9th, clergymen, kindred on the wife's side, etc., and so on with the other houses ; the stronger the ruler of these houses so much more formidable will be his enemies ; but note, if ♃ or ♀ be in any house, and befriends the querent's significator, then they portend good ; thus, suppose lord of 3rd afflicts lord of 1st, and ♃ be in the 3rd, they would then denote that brethren or neighbours would be some *enemies*, and some *friends*, and the positions of the lord of 3rd and ♃ would show respectively the description of persons who were friendly or unfriendly disposed towards the querent.

OF LIQUIDATION

11. *Shall I be able to liquidate by arrangement ?*— The 1st is for the querent, and the 7th for his creditors, if these lords be in good aspect, or lord of 1st dispose of lord of 7th, and the lord of 1st not afflicted by ♅, ♄, or ♂, *you can ;* but if the lord of 1st be disposed of by lord of 7th, or lord of 7th afflicts the lord of 1st, or ♅, ♄, or ♂ be in he 7th, you *cannot*, but your creditors will seek to ruin you, or sell you off, or force you into the bankruptcy court. *Proceedings in bankruptcy may be judged the same as for lawsuits.*

OF WAR

12. *Shall I return from the war ?*—The 1st is for the querent, and the 7th for the war, if the lord of the 7th afflicts the lord of the 1st or the ☽ ; the lord of the 1st in the 8th or 4th, or afflicted by ♂ or ♄, or the ☽ afflicted in the 8th by ♄ or ♂, he will be killed ; if you find the aforesaid evil positions, yet ♃ beholds the ☽ or lord of ascendant by ⚼, ✶, or △, the querent will be wounded, but not killed.   If ♅ afflicts he will suffer from explosions ; an evil planet, and if lord of the 7th or 8th, in the 1st, a bad token ; the lord of the 12th afflicting the lord of the 1st, he will be taken prisoner.   The ☽ *well aspected* by ♂ shows courage and slight wounds ;   *afflicted* by ♂, serious wounds ;   if by ♄, he is in danger of dying from his wounds, the same if the ☉ be afflicted by ♄, and in the 8th.   The lord of the 1st in the 10th, strong, denotes honour, and a safe return ;   the same if the lord of the 1st be in good aspect of ☉, ☽, and ♃, and not afflicted by the lord of 7th or 8th ;   the lord of the 1st cadent shows he will not distinguish himself, and scarcely do his duty ;   angular, that he will be praised, and if in good aspect of ☉ will receive a medal for his conduct, and be in favour with the General.

13. *Will two armies fight ?*—If the lords of 1st and 7th be going to ⚼, ☐, or ☍ in angles, they will fight severely ;   if in succeedent houses, a sharp battle ;   if in cadent houses, there will be little fighting.   The day they will fight can be judged by the time the aspect is *actually formed*, and not by the number of degrees between the two significators.

OF STOCKS AND SHARES

14. *Of stocks, shares, etc.*—Have regard to the lords of the 1st and 2nd, and the Moon, if you find the ☽ separating from a good aspect of the lord of the 8th, and applying to a good aspect of the lord of 2nd, you may buy ; if you find the lord of the 8th disposed of by the lord of tpe 2nd, and the lord of the 2nd in good aspect to the ☽, ♃, or ♀, you may either *buy* or *sell* ; never buy when there is a malefic in the 1st, 2nd, 7th, or 8th, unless it be lord of the 1st or 2nd, also if the lord of the 7th be afflicting the lord of 1st or 2nd, do not buy ; but if the ruler of the 2nd afflicts the lord of the 8th, you may buy or sell ; the lord of the 7th in the 2nd, you are sure to lose.

The time when to buy.—See when the lord of the 2nd is in good aspect to, or disposes of, the lord of the 8th, or the ☽ translates the light from the lord of the 8th to the lord of the 2nd, and at that time *buy ;* the hour must be taken when the lord of the 2nd reaches by *diurnal* motion the cusp of the 8th house ; it is also a good time to buy when the ☽ is separating from the lord of the 8th by an *evil* aspect, and applying to lord of 2nd by a *good* aspect.

When to sell.—Let a benefic occupy the 2nd house, and let the lord of the 1st be in the 7th, and the ☽ going from a good aspect of the lord of 2nd, to a bad aspect of the lords of 7th or 8th, and the hour when these aspects are formed, or the lord of the 1st gets in the 7th by *diurnal* motion, is the time to sell. Much experience is required in questions of this kind.

NOTE.—If a person applies to you to either buy or sell some shares you must take the 1st and 2nd for him, and the 7th and 8th for yourself, and judge as already taught.

OF MARRIAGE

15. *Shall I marry ?*—For *women* take the lord of the 1st and the ☉ ; for *men*, the lord of the 1st and the ☽ ; if you find these significators in good aspect to ♃ or ♀ ; or these planets occupy the 5th or 7th houses or the lord of the 1st in the 5th, 7th, or 11th houses ; the lords of the 1st or 7th in good aspect or going to ☌ ; a fruitful sign on 5th, 7th, or 11th, are all strong

testimonies of marriage ; the lord of the 7th in the 1st, another testimony ; if the lord of the 1st, or a luminary, apply by evil aspect to ♄, ♂, or ♅, and these planets occupy the 5th or 7th, and there be no help from ♃ or ♀, then the querent will not marry ; if the signs on the 5th, 7th or 11th be barren, there is doubt, unless ♃, ♀, ☉, or ☽ be in either house ; but before pronouncing *against* marriage, look well to every significator, and the quality of the sign it is in, and the quality of the signs that occupy the cusps of the 1st, 5th, 7th, and 11th houses.

16. *Shall I marry my present lover ?*—If the lord of the 1st or the 7th be going to a ♂, ✳, or △ aspect, or in *mutual reception*, or the lord of the 1st in the 7th, and that light which is co-significator of the querent (*viz.,* ☽) for a man, and ☉ for a woman), in favourable aspect, or ♂, to the lord of the 1st or 7th, you will marry your present lover ; but if the rulers of the 1st or 7th *refrain* from forming a good aspect or are *separating ;* the lords of the 1st or 7th in ☐ or ☍ of the co-significator ; the malefics receiving the rays of either significator, and afflicted ; the luminaries in ill aspect ; these all show a breaking off of the engagement.

17. *The cause of the disagreement.*—If the significators or co-significators are applying to each other by friendly aspect, and another planet interposes, then the marriage will fall through, and the house ruled or occupied by this third planet shows from where the trouble will come ; if it be the lord of the 2nd or 8th, it will be on account of money; if the 3rd or 9th, through brethren or neighbours ; the 4th or 10th, parents will interpose and prevent it ; 5th or 11th, children, morality, friends, etc.; 6th or 12th, sickness, uncles or aunts, secret enemies, etc., as signified by these houses.

18. *When shall I marry ?*—Judge this by the number of degrees the significators lack in completing the ♂, ✳, or △ aspect ; or the lord of the 7th

or ☽ to ♀ or ☉, or the co-significator to either lord of 1st or 7th.

19. *Shall I be happy in marriage ?*—The lord of the 1st in good aspect to ♃ or ♀, or the ☽, ♃, or ♀ in the 7th, unafflicted ; the lords of the 1st or 7th in good aspect or *mutual reception*, you will be happy and agree ; but if you find the malefics in the 7th, the lord of the 7th afflicting the lord of the 1st, and there be no *agreement* or *translation* between these lords, you will not be happy, but there will be much quarrelling and unpleasantness ; the same if the cusps of these houses are moveable, and their lords in moveable signs. Evil planets in the 7th afflicting the lord of the 1st, denote the mischief will arise from the wife or husband ; if these malefics be in the 1st, the querent is to blame ; if the affliction comes from the 4th or 10th, or from the lords of these houses, the parents will cause continual bother; if from the 6th, by means of servants and low people ; from the 5th or 11th, through immorality ; if ♅ afflicts, jealousy, and one of the party will go astray ; the ☉ or ☽ afflicted by ♅, ♄, or ♂, the parties will not agree or be happy.

20. *Shall I marry a stranger ?*—The lord of the 7th cadent, in the 3rd or 9th, you will ; but if in the 7th or 1st, then you will marry one whom you know well. If the lord of seventh be in angles, you will *know* him or her ; if in succeedent houses, you often *see* him or her, but are not acquainted.

21. *Shall I gain by marriage ?*—♃ or ♀ in the 8th, or the lord of the 8th strong in the 8th, the lord of the 8th strong, and in good aspect of the lord of the 2nd, you will gain by marriage, but if you find the lord of the 8th weak or afflicted, and out of dignities, there will be no gain.

22. *Shall I marry more than once ?*—If the lord of the 1st be in double-bodied sign, or if it apply to many planets at the same time, or if double-bodied signs occupy the 5th or 7th, you will ; but if the lord of

the ascendant be in fixed signs, or aspect only one planet, or if the ☽ (for a man) or the ☉ (for a woman) aspect only one planet, you will marry but once.

23. *Who will be the best situated of the two ?*—See which ruler is the strongest, best placed, or better aspected ; if the lord of the 7th, the husband or wife will be better off, or in a better position than the querent ; but if the lord of the 1st be the strongest, then the querent will be the better off.

24. *Has my sweetheart another lover ?* If the lord of the 7th be in ☌, ⚹, or △ of any planet except the lord of the 1st, she has ; also if several planets be in the 7th, or ☉ in aspect to ♂ or ♅, or applying to the ☌ of ♃ ; the planet the lord of the 7th applies to, will describe the person to whom she is attached ; as if ♂, an engineer, soldier, officer, contractor, etc. ; ♃, a merchant, lawyer, or professional person ; ♄, an old man or elderly person ; ♅, a mechanic or author ; ☿, a writer, clerk, or book-keeper ; the sign occupied by any of these planets will describe him and his dress ; but if you find the lord of 7th in aspect to the lord of 1st, void of course, or if there be no planet in the 7th, and the ☉ be not in aspect to any planet but the lord of the 1st, she has not another lover.

25. *Has my lover another sweetheart ?*—Judge exactly as above, but instead of the ☉ take the ☽, and if you find her or the lord of the 7th in any aspect to any planet but the lord of the 1st, he has ; especially if ☽ be in ☌, ⚹, or △ of ♂ or ♅, and either not lord of the 7th ; the description of person, etc., may be seen as described in question 22.

26. *Who will live the longest ?*—The lords of the 1st and 8th are for the querent's death, with the ☽ as *co-significator ;* the lords of the 7th and 2nd denote the husband or wife, and his or her death. See whose significator is the strongest of the two, angular, and especially free from going to combustion, not ℞,

cadent, or afflicted by the lords of the 6th or 8th, and that party will live the longest ; if the testimonies are about equal, then neither will long survive the other ; the significator going to combustion, or to affliction by the lord of the 8th, or the ☽ similarly placed, is a bad sign for the querent's life, or the quesited's life, if the lord of the 7th be similarly placed.

27. *Will my husband return to me ?*—See where the lord of the 7th is, if ℞, and applying to lord of 1st, or in the 1st, or a translation of light between the lords of 1st and 7th, or the ☽ applying by good aspect to the lord of the 1st, he returns ; the lord of the 7th combust, or afflicted by the infortunes, he will be found against his will ; but the lord of the 7th cadent, swift, and unafflicted, he will not return ; lord of 7th in good aspect of ♃ or ♀, or leaving combustion he will not be found.

28. *Will my wife return to me ?*—Judge exactly as shown in question 25 ; the location of the absconded party, and his or her condition, can be judged from the position of the lord of the 7th ; also his distance from the house, as shown in the judgment for absconded children, chapter v., question 8.

29. *Describe my husband or wife.*—Look to the 7th house, if you find a planet there, see what sign it is in, and that planet and sign will describe your future partner. If no planet be in the 7th, see what sign the lord of the 7th is in, and judge according to the descriptions given in Part I, chap. iii.

OF THEFTS

In all cases of theft, the lord of the 1st denotes the querent ; the 2nd house and its ruler denote the thing stolen ; the 4th and its ruler show the place where the article then is ; the 7th, its lord, or a peregrine planet therein, or in any angle, or the 2nd house, shows the thief.

30. *Are the goods mislaid or stolen ?*—If the ☽ be ruler of the 1st and in the 4th, and the lord of the 2nd in the 4th, they are *hidden* ; if ☽ be in the 2nd, and going to ☌ of lord of 7th, they are *mislaid* ; the ruler of the 7th in the 1st, and disposed of by the ☽, they are not stolen, but *misplaced* ; but if the ☽, or lord of the 1st or 2nd, be in ☌, or afflict the lord of the 7th, or ♅, ♄, or ♂ be in the 1st or 2nd, or lord of 1st peregrine, they are stolen.

If you find they are *not* stolen, but hidden or mislaid, refer to chapter iv., Part II., question 11, and judge as therein described.

31. *Who is the thief ?*—The lord of the 7th in the 1st, 4th, 5th, 6th, 7th, or 10th, it is a person of the household, also if the lord of the 1st and 7th be in one house ; if the lord of the 7th or peregrine planet be in the 1st, there is reason to suspect the querent himself ; in the 2nd, his wife, sweetheart, or maid-servant ; in the 3rd, a brother, sister, cousin, or neighbour ; 4th, a father, or an old man ; 5th, children or young persons, messengers ; 6th, servants, tenants, or lodgers ; 7th, a person with whom he deals, or one who comes to the house, his wife or sweetheart ; in the 8th, a servant who sometimes frequents the house ; the 9th, a stranger, some tramp who sells religious tracts, or one who affects religion, or his wife's kindred ; the 10th, a superior person, or master ; 11th, a friend, or one who has done the querent a service ; 12th, some vagabond who has been in prison. The lord of the 7th in the 8th, 9th, or 12th, frequently shows *strangers*.

32. *The description of the thief.*—See in what sign the significator of the thief is placed, and refer to Part I., chap. iii. ; the *disposition* of the thief depends much on how his significator is aspected.

33. *Are there more than one thief ?*—If the angles are *fixed*, and the significator of the thief in a fixed sign, and in no aspect to any planet in the 2nd, there is only one ; but if many planets afflict the lord of 2nd,

or ☽, or the significator of the thief be in a double-bodied sign, or in aspect to many planets, then there are more than one.

34. *Is the thief male or female ?*—♅, ♄, ♃, ♂, ☉, or ☿ shows a *male* ; ☽ and ♀ a *female* ; ♅ and ♄ denote old men above the age of 50 ; ♃ and ♂ from 40 to 50 ; ☉ from 25 to 40 ; ☿ a young person, probably under 20 ; the ☽ denotes married and elderly females ; ♀ young and single females. Some say the *quarters* of the ☽ denote the age, thus : her first, quarter *very young* ; second quarter, from 20 to 30, etc. ; but this I do not regard, for if so, all the robberies committed in seven days must be by similarly aged persons ! *Do not rely too much upon the ages signified by the planets, as every aspect formed to the thief's significator alters them.*

35. *Which way is the thief ?*—The significator of the thief in the different houses and signs will show the way he has gone (see Part I). If the significator be angular, he is near or in the house still ; in succeedent houses, a little way off, or about the out premises ; if cadent, he is far off ; the ☽ similarly placed signifies the same. Also, if the thief's significator be going out of one sign into another, he is about to change his direction, or go off another way ; if in watery signs, and in bad aspect of ♀, he is drinking ; and if the property stolen be money, he is making off with it fast.

36. *The thief's door.*—The ☽ in a fixed sign, one door to the house ; in a common sign, two doors ; if in a moveable sign, there are steps up to the door ; if ♄ aspects the ☽, it is a very old door, and has been mended ; if ♂, there is iron about the outside ; if the ☽ be under the earth, the door is at the back of the house ; if above, in the front ; if just rising or setting, the door is at the side.

37. *Will the thief be taken ?*—The lord of the 7th or 8th in the 1st, or ☌ of lord of 1st ; the ☽ rising in △ to lord of 1st ; ☽ in 7th applying to □ of ♂, ☉, or ☿, or separating from these planets and applying to □ of

⊙ ; lord of 7th afflicted, or going to combustion of the ⊙ ; the ☽ or lord of 7th joined to an evil planet, *he will be taken*. But if the lord of 7th be swift in motion, in a moveable sign and cadent, in good aspect to ♃, ♀, or ☽, he will not be taken ; also see what house the lord of 7th is in, as in the 11th he will be assisted in his escape by friends ; in the 12th by means of servants ; in the 3rd by strangers ; in the 10th he will hide himself ; in the 4th he will go about publicly ; in the 9th by means of brethren or neighbours.

38. *Does the thief still possess the property ?*—If the thief's significator be in good aspect of any benevolent planet, and at the same time dispose of another *fortune*, they are then in his hands ; but otherwise they are sold or disposed of.

39. *Will the goods be recovered ?*—The lord of the 8th in the ascendant, or with the lord of the ascendant, or the lord of the 7th in the 8th, shows recovery ; if ⊙ and ☽ behold the ascendant, the articles will be recovered ; the same if the lord of 2nd be in the 1st, or lord of 1st in the 2nd, or lord of 1st in 7th or 8th, or lord of 2nd in the 4th or 11th ; the luminaries both in the 10th denote *sudden* recovery ; the lord of the 7th combust, or turning ℞, the thief brings them back, especially if applying to lord of ascendant, or 2nd ; the ☽ with ♃ or ♀ in the 2nd, a *good sign* ; but if you find the malefics out of their dignities in the 2nd ; the lord of the 2nd afflicted in the 8th, or by the lord of the 8th ; the lords of 7th and 8th in ☌ ; the lights not in aspect to each other ; the thief's ruler afflicting the ☽ ; the lord of the 7th strong and unafflicted ; the lights under the earth ; they all show that the goods will not be recovered. *Where the figure is not clear, it is always best to make a list of the testimonies for and against, and judge by the majority, as it is frequently difficult to balance them accurately in the mind.*

40. *When shall I recover the stolen articles ?*—If you find testimony that the goods will be recovered,

8

observe the application of the planets that signify the recovery, and see the number of degrees before they make perfect aspects, and then judge of the time by the Measure of Time on page 46.

41. *Of the nature of the goods stolen.*—This is shown by the lord of the 2nd house, and judged the same as for articles lost or mislaid in chapter iv, question 11.

42. *The dress of the thief.*—The sign and house occupied by the significator of the thief, and the colour ruled by his significator, will show the colour of his dress.

CHAPTER IX

OF QUESTIONS RELATING TO THE EIGHTH HOUSE

1. *Will there be a death in the family soon ?*—♅, ♄, or ♂ in the 8th, there will ; also if the lord of the 3rd, 4th, 8th, or 10th, be much afflicted ; but if none of these testimonies are present, then judge in the negative.

2. *Who will be the first to die in the family ?*—Have regard to the 1st, 3rd, 4th, 5th, 7th, and 10th houses, and whichever ruler is the most afflicted, that member will die first ; as the ruler of the 3rd, a brother ; 4th, a father ; 10th, a mother ; 5th, a child ; 1st, the querent himself ; 7th, his wife, etc.

3. *Shall I have a legacy left me ?*—The lord of the 8th strong, and in good aspect to the lord of the 2nd ; the lord of the 8th in the 8th ; ♃ or ♀ strong in the 8th, and in friendly aspect to the lord of the 2nd ; ♃ in the 8th strong ; in ✳ or △ to ♄ or ♅, you will ; but ♄, ♅, ♂ weak in the 8th, or the lord of the 8th weak or, afflicting lord of the 2nd, and without *reception* or *translation*, you will *not* get a legacy.

4. *Shall I obtain my wife's or husband's portion ?*— If the lord of the 8th be not weak, impeded, or afflicted by ♅, ♄, or ♂, and if ♃ or ♀ be on the 8th cusp, and the lords of the 8th and 2nd, in *reception*,

or *friendly* aspect, or if there be *translation of light* between the lords of 8th and 2nd, you will get it ; but if the lords of the 1st or 2nd be afflicted by lord of 8th, or the latter weak, afflicted, combust, ℞, or peregrine, you will get nothing, or but little at the very most.

5. *Will my wife's portion be good or not ?*—If you find ♃ or ♀ in the 8th, and the lord of the 8th strong and well placed, the wife will have money ; but if the lord of 8th be afflicted, combust, cadent, or ℞, she will have no portion ; and if you find a benefic strong in the 8th, in ☐ or ☍ to a malefic, there is danger that the querent's wife will be done out of her portion.

The above question will serve for a woman as well as a man, and, in fact, will discover the position of any person as regards money, unless it be a relative or friend.

CHAPTER X

OF QUESTIONS RELATING TO THE NINTH HOUSE

1. *Of a voyage at sea.*—The lord of the 9th strong, and well aspected, and the lord of the ascendant free from evil, and no malefic in the 9th, the voyage will be safe and prosperous. If a fortune be in the 10th, he will meet success on the voyage ; in if the 7th, a good reception to where he is going ; but if you find ♅, ♄, or ♂ in the 9th, or the lord of the 9th afflicted, combust, or ℞, the querent will meet with no success, and return without accomplishing his desires. Evil planets in the 8th are bad for success, and denote but little gain, and the 10th house or its lord afflicted, he will gain but little credit or esteem by the voyage.

2. *Shall I do well in a foreign land ?*—The 9th house and its lord strong and unafflicted, and favourably disposed towards the lord of the 1st or 2nd, or the lord of 1st or 2nd strong and well aspected in the 9th, and the ☽ *angular* and *unafflicted*, the querent would succeed ; but the lord of the 4th stronger, and better

placed and aspected than the lord of the 9th, he will do better in his native land.

3. *What does my dream signify ?*—If ♅ was near the cusp of the 9th, it was a most strange and uncommon dream ; if ♄, it was melancholy and frightful ; ♂, fighting, quarrelling, war, etc. Now, if the lord of the 9th afflicts the lord of 1st, the dream denotes trouble to the querent's person and health ; if the lord of 2nd, his money will suffer ; if the lord of 5th, his children, and so on of the other houses. But if the lord of 9th be in friendly aspect to any of these lords, then the dream portends good ; the same if a benefic occupies the 9th house and is in favourable aspect to the lord of 1st.

I advise the student only to set figures when the dream is important, or very uncommon, or when it leaves a remarkable impression on the mind, it then denotes a something, which the figure will show.

4. *Shall I be able to insure ?*—The lords of 1st and 9th, or ☽, in bad aspect, or the lord of 7th afflicting lord of 1st or 2nd, or in no aspect, then you will not succeed ; but if friendly testimonies exist between these significators, you will be able to effect an insurance. But if the lord of 7th or 8th be an infortune, and in the 2nd, be wary, for you will suffer from the company.

5. *Shall I gain by learning or science ?*—The lords of the 1st and 9th in ☌, ✳, or △, or ♃ or ♀ in the 9th, strong, in good aspect to the lord of the ascendant, the ☽ in ✳ to the lord of the 9th, and ♅ in ✳ or △ to ☽ or ☿ in the 9th, the querent will prosper, and delight in learning, but if the lord of the 9th be weak and afflicted, or afflicts the lord of 1st or 2nd, or ♄ or ♂ be lord of the 9th, and afflicted by position, he will benefit nothing, and will not succeed in his study.

6. *Shall I benefit by publishing anything ?*—This question is judged similarly to question 5. Good planets in the 9th, in △ to ☿ in the 1st, or ☿ essentially strong in the 9th or in the 10th, and the ☽ in △, expect

benefit; but if ☿ or lord of the 9th be in the 6th, 12th, or 8th, or much afflicted, no benefit will be obtained, and the querent will do well to relinquish his ideas.

CHAPTER XI

OF QUESTIONS RELATING TO THE TENTH HOUSE

1. *Shall I succeed in business ?*—If you find the ☽ and the lords of the 1st and 10th in good aspect, and the *lights* with the *fortunes* ; ♃, ☉, ☽, or ♀ in the 10th, strong and unafflicted, and in favourable aspect to the lord of the 1st or 2nd, *you will prosper*; but if you find many planets cadent, or the benefics cadent and the infortunes angular, and especially in the 10th or 2nd, you will not do well. A figure for a question of this nature must be judged in a *general* way, and not too much stress laid on any house (except the 10th), or its significator; but if the ☉, ☽, and ♃ are in favourable aspect and angular, he is sure to succeed, but not so if the malefics hold prominent positions.

2. *What kind of business had I better follow ?*—If the lord of the 10th, or a planet in the 10th, be in ♈, he will do well as a cattle-dealer, groom, grazier, veterinary surgeon, carpenter, or coachbuilder; if in ♉, farming, gardening, corn-dealing; if in ♊, writer, clerk, painter, surveyor, or schoolmaster; if in ♋, the sea, or publican, brewer, wine-merchant, etc.; if in ♌, a jockey, smith, watchmaker, huntsman, or cow-doctor; in ♍, a secretary, stationer, printer, or accountant; in ♎, singer, linen-draper, tailor, silk-mercer, or fancy-draper; in ♏, surgeon, apothecary, brazier, founder, brewer, waterman, or maltster; in ♐, cattle-dealer, clergyman, sportsman, or horse-doctor; in ♑, chandler, grocer, farmer, dealer in wool, lead, or corn; in ♒, carpenter, painter, sculptor, or merchant; in ♓, brewer, fishmonger, jester, singer, waiter in taverns, wine-merchant, or publican.

3. *Shall I obtain the promotion or situation ?*—The
lords of the 1st and 10th, in ✶ or △ ; the ☉ in ✶ or
△ to lord of 1st ; the ☉ or ☽ ruler of the 10th, and
the lord of 1st received by them ; lord of 10th in 1st ;
☽ separating from lord of 10th, and applying to lord
of 1st ; lord of 1st disposing of lord of 10th ; lord of
1st *angular, strong,* and in good aspect to the ☉, ☽,
or ♃ ; lord of 1st the first planet the lord of 10th
aspects ; these all show that the situation or promotion will be obtained ; but if the lord of 10th, or
☉, afflicts lord of 1st or 2nd or ☽ ; or lord of 1st *weak*
and afflicted ; lord of 10th applying by ✶ or △ to the
lord of 7th, expect a *disappointment.* The same if ♄
be angular, and afflicts the ☽ or the lord of ascendant.

4. *Shall I remain long in my present place ?*—Lords
of 1st and 10th in good aspect, in *fixed* or common
signs and angles ; or lord of 1st in good aspect of ♃,
♀, or ☉, and not afflicted by the infortunes, it will be
long before he leaves.   The same if lord of 1st be in
the 10th, or *vice versa.*

5. *When shall I leave my present employer ?*—If the
lord of the 10th or the ☽, are disposed of by any planet
in any angle (except the 4th), and that planet be slow
in motion, he will not leave until that planet be combust, or ℞, or leave the sign he is then in ; also, see
when the lord of the 10th leaves the sign he is then
in, and about that time the querent changes.

6. *Will it be well to leave this situation ?*—The lords
of the 10th and 1st strong, in good aspect, or *reception,
angular,* and *unafflicted,* do not leave ; but if lord of
10th be weak, cadent and afflicted ; or if the planet
the ☉ next meets by ☌, ✶, or △, be a *benefic,* you
may move.

7. *What will be the cause of my leaving ?*—The lord
of 1st combust, you have annoyed your master ; if
you find the lord of 1st *afflicted* by any planet, and
this planet in the 10th, or in friendly aspect to the ☉
or lord of 10th, you will suffer by a person signified
by that planet, and the house he governs, and his

locality, will show the person who has done you the injury ; if the lord of the 2nd, it will have to do with money, cash, etc. ; the lord of 3rd with letters or rumours from neighbours, damaging to yourself, and so on of the other houses.

8. *Contracts for work, etc.*—The lords of the 10th and 2nd in good aspect ; the ☉ in good aspect to lord of 2nd ; the lord of the 1st strong in the 11th ; or ♃, ♀, ☉, or ☽ well aspected in the 10th, the work will pay you to take ; but if the lords of the 10th and 2nd be afflicted, or cadent, or these houses occupied by the malefics, you will gain neither money nor credit by the job.

CHAPTER XII

OF QUESTIONS RELATING TO THE ELEVENTH HOUSE

1. *If I shall obtain the thing hoped for.*—Good aspects between the lords of 1st and 11th, or *reception*, or *translation of light*, he will ; or if the lord of 11th be in the 1st, and the ☽ well aspected, he will ; but if the aspect between the lords of 1st and 11th, be by □, but with *reception*, he will obtain it with *difficulty*. Evil planets in the 1st or 11th, and ☽ afflicted, or cadent, he will not obtain it.

2. *Is my friend true or false ?*—Good planets in the 11th in good aspect to the lord of the 1st, and lord of 11th a good planet, he is true ; but if ♅, ♄, or ♂ be in the 11th, or rules this house, and afflicts the ascendant, he is *false* ; ☿ afflicted in the 11th, he is *not* to be *trusted*.

3. *Describe the person who is my best friend.*—See if a good planet occupy the 11th, if so, judge by it and the sign it is in ; or if the lord of the 11th *befriends* the lord of the 1st, judge by it, and the sign it is in.

NOTE.—If a malefic occupy the 11th, and the lord of the 11th be also a malefic, he has no friend he can trust.

CHAPTER XIII

OF QUESTIONS RELATING TO THE TWELFTH HOUSE

1. *Of Imprisonment.*—If ☽ be *swift in motion*, in a *moveable* sign, or lord of ascendant, or ☽ separating from the lord of the 4th, or applying to a fortune, a speedy release ; a *moveable* sign on cusp of 12th, and its lord in a moveable sign, a speedy release ; but if this lord occupies a *fixed* sign, and the ☽ be *cadent* and *fixed*, the lord of the 1st in the 4th, 6th, 8th, or 12th, the lord of the ascendant combust, or ℞, afflicted, or " fixed," a long imprisonment.

2. *Have I private enemies ?*—A malefic in the 12th, or lord of 12th a malefic, you have ; and if it afflicts lord of 1st or 2nd, he is doing you harm.   Benefics in the 12th, or its lord a benefic, you have nothing to fear from private foes.

3. *Describe my private foes.*—See the sign occupied by the malefics in the 12th, or the sign holding the lord of 12th, and judge the foe by the description it gives, and his condition and strength may be judged by the situation of the lord of 12th, or a malefic in the 12th ; if in its own *house*, the foe is very powerful, and if the planet be elevated above the querent's significator, and in ill aspect thereto, he *can* and *will* do him *harm* ; but if the aspect be by ✶ or △, then *he can*, but *will not* do the querent injury.

CHAPTER XIV

EXPLANATION OF TERMS USED IN HORARY ASTROLOGY

Affliction.—A planet being in evil aspect to any planet or ☌ to a malefic, cadent, or in its debilities.

Angles.—The four houses which commence at the points where the ☉ rises, culminates, sets, and arrives at midnight, viz., the east, south, west, and north, or the 1st, 4th, 7th, and 10th houses.

Application.—The approaching of one planet to another, or to the cusp of any house, either by ☌ or aspect.

Ascendant.—The eastern horizon, or the cusp of that house which represents the party, as the cusp of the 5th is the ascendant for a *child* of the *querent.*

Barren Signs.—♊, ♌, and ♍.

Benefics.—The two planets ♃ and ♀.

Bestial Signs.—♈, ♉, ♌, ♐ (the first half excepted), and ♑.

Besieged.—A planet being placed between two others.

Cadent.—Falling from an angle ; these are the 3rd, 6th, 9th, and 12th houses.

Collection of Light.—When the planet receives the aspects of any two others which are not themselves in aspect.   It denotes that the affair will be forwarded by a third person described by that planet, but not unless they both receive him in some of their dignities.

Combustion.—Being within 8° 30′ of the ☉, which is said to burn up those planets near him, so that they lose their power.   It is always an evil testimony.

Conjunction.—Two planets being in the same longitude.   If they be exactly in the same degree and minute, it is a *partile* conjunction, and very powerful.

Cusp.—The beginning of any house.

Decreasing in Light.—When any planet is past the ☍ of ☉, it decreases in light ;   the ☽ so placed is not a good sign.

Detriment.—The sign opposite the house of any planet ; as ♂ in ♎ is in his detriment.   It is a sign of weakness, debility, etc.

Dignities.—These are either essential or accidental. The former are when any planet is in its own house, exaltation, or triplicity ;   the latter are when any planet is in an angle, and well aspected, not afflicted,

swift in motion, increasing in light, etc.   The reverse
of dignities is debilities.

Direct.—When any planet moves on in the regular
order of the signs, from ♈ towards ♉, etc.

Dispose, Dispositor.—A planet disposes of any other
which may be found in its essential dignities, thus : if
☉ be in ♈, the house of ♂, then ♂ disposes of ☉, and
is said to rule, receive, or govern him.   When the
dispositor of the planet signifying the thing asked
after is himself disposed of by the lord of the ascendant, it is a good sign.   To dispose by house is the
most powerful testimony, then by exaltation, then
triplicity.

Double-bodied Signs.—♊, ♐, ♓.

Earthy Signs.—♉, ♍, and ♑, which form the
earthy triplicity.

Exaltation.—An essential dignity, next in power to
that of house.

Fall.—A planet is in fall when in the sign opposite
to its exaltation.   It shows a person in a weak and
hopeless state, unless the planet be well aspected.

Familiarity.—Any kind of aspect or reception.

Feminine Signs.—These are all the even signs,
reckoning from Aries, ♉, ♋, ♍, ♏, ♑, and ♓.

Fiery Signs, or Fiery Triplicity.—♈, ♌, ♐.

Figure.—The diagram which represents the heavens
at any time.   It is also called a scheme, horoscope,
map, etc.

Fortunes.—♃ and ♀, and the ☉, ☽, and ☿, if
aspecting them, and not afflicted, are considered
fortunate planets.

Fruitful Signs.—♋, ♏, and ♓.

Frustration.—The cutting off, or preventing anything shown by one aspect by means of another—
thus : if ♀, lady of the ascendant, were hastening to
the △ of ♂, lord of the 7th, in a question of marriage,
it might denote that the match would take place ;
but if ☿ were to form an ☍ to ♂ before ♀ reached her
△ of that planet, it would be a frustration, and would

show that the hopes of the querent would be cut off ; and if ☿ were lord of the 12th, it might denote that it would be done by a private enemy.

Houses.—The twelve divisions or compartments into which the circle of the heavens is divided ; also the signs in which any planet is said to have most influence.

Human Signs.—♊, ♍, ♒, and the first half of ♐ Any person's significator therein, shows them to be of a humane disposition.

Impedited.—This signifies being afflicted by evil stars. The ☽ is impedited in the highest degree when in ☌ with ☉.

Joined to.—Being in any aspect.

Increasing in Light.—When any planet is leaving ☉ and is not yet arrived at the ☍ ; after which it decreases in light. The former is a good, the latter an evil, testimony, but chiefly as regards the ☽.

Increasing in Motion.—Where any planet moves faster than it did on the preceding day.

Infortunes.—♅, ♄, and ♂ ; also ☿ when he is much afflicted.

Intercepted.—A sign which is found between the cusps of two houses.

Lights.—The ☉ and ☽.

Lord.—That planet whose house is occupied by any other, is said to be the lord or ruler of that other ; and if his sign be on the cusp of any house, he is called the lord of that house. Thus, if ♈ ascend in any figure, ♂ who rules that sign, is the lord of the ascendant.

Masculine Signs.—They are odd signs, viz., the 1st, 3rd, 5th, etc., or ♈, ♊, ♌, ♎, ♐, ♒.

Meridian.—The midheaven, or place where ☉ is at noon. The opposite point, or where ☉ is at midnight, is the cusp of the 4th house, or the meridian under the earth.

Moveable Signs.—♈, ♋, ♎, and ♑.

Orb.—That distance round a planet to which its influence more particularly extends.

Oriental.—Planets found between the 4th house and the midheaven, rising, are in the eastern half of the figure, and said to be oriental. When they have passed the midheaven, and until they reach the 4th again, they are occidental.

Peregrine.—Having no essential dignity whatever. A planet is not reckoned peregrine that is in mutual reception with any other.

Querent.—The person who queries or inquires.

Quesited.—The person or thing inquired about.

Radical.—That which belongs to the radix, or root, fit to be judged.

Reception.—The being received by any planet as being in that planet's essential dignities ; it is a good testimony when *mutual.* See *Dispose.*

Refranation.—When two planets are coming to any aspect, and one falls *retrograde* before the aspect is complete. It denotes that the matter will wholly fail.

Retrograde.—When any planet is decreasing in longitude. It is a very great debility.

Separation.—When any aspect is past, but is yet within orbs, the planets are said to separate from each other. It denotes that the influence is passing away.

Significator.—The planet which is lord of the house which rules the matter inquired after. The lord of the ascendant is the general significator of the querent. The ☽ is in general his consignificator.

Signs of Long Ascension.—♋, ♌, ♍, ♎, ♏, ♐.

Signs of Short Ascension.—♑, ♒, ♓, ♈, ♉, ♊.

Swift in Motion.—When a planet moves faster than its mean motion.

Testimony.—Having any aspect or dignity, etc., or being in any way in operation in the figure as regards the question asked.

Translation of Light.—The conveying the influence of one planet to another, by separating from the aspect of one and going to the other. It is a very powerful testimony.

Triplicity.—An essential dignity. The zodiac is

divided into four trigons or triplicities—the fiery, ♈︎, ♌︎, ♐︎ ; the earthy, ♉︎, ♍︎, ♑︎ ; the airy, ♊︎, ♎︎, ♒︎ ; the watery, ♋︎, ♏︎, and ♓︎ ; agreeing with the four elements into which the ancients divided the whole of the natural world.

Void of Course.—Forming no aspect in the sign it is in. When the ☽ is so, it denotes in general no success in the question.

Watery Signs.—♋︎, ♏︎, and ♓︎.

Watery Triplicity.—♋︎, ♏︎, ♓︎.